The British Columbia Columbia Seasonal Cookbook

Jennifer Ogle
Eric Pateman
James Darcy

Lone Pine Publishing

The Publisher: Lone Pine Publishing
10145–81 Avenue
Edmonton, AB, Canada T6E 1W9
Website: www.lonepinepublishing.com

Library and Archives Canada Cataloguing in Publication
Ogle, Jennifer, 1972–
   The B.C. seasonal cookbook / Jennifer Ogle, Eric Pateman, James Darcy.

Includes index.
ISBN 13: 978-1-55105-584-8
ISBN 10: 1-55105-584-8

   1. Cookery, Canadian--British Columbia style.
I. Pateman, Eric, 1974– II. Title.

TX715.6.O4517 2007   641.59711   C2007-901377-5

Editorial Director: Nancy Foulds
Editorial: Carol Woo, Sandra Bit
Production Manager: Gene Longson
Book Design and Layout: Willa Kung, Elliot Engley, Heather Markham
Cover Design: Gerry Dotto

Food Stylists: Jennifer Ogle, Ernest Sternal

All photographs by Nanette Samol, except those on p. 16, 46, 50, 52, 54, 56, 60, 96, 98, 130, 152, 156 by Merle Prosofsky.

Special thanks to Lovoni Walker for her recipe and food styling for Smoked Salmon with Asparagus Salad, p. 22 and front cover.

Thank you to the following people who assisted with our photo shoots: Alison Beck, Laura Peters, Lori Holowaychuk, Mary Lobay.

We acknowledge the financial support of the Government of Canada through the Book Publishing Industry Development Program (BPIDP) for our publishing activities.

PC: P14

CONTENTS

DEDICATION

This book is dedicated to all the farmers and artisan producers in the wonderful province of British Columbia who inspire all of us at Edible B.C. each and every day.

For Ernest
Dziękuję kochanej.
JO

INTRODUCTION

British Columbia is blessed with abundant farmland, the vast waters of the Pacific Ocean, pristine inland lakes and streams, as well as the climate and conditions to produce a wide variety of food. Local farms produce meats, eggs, vegetables, fruits and grains. Artisans and small producers offer almost every imaginable food—from cheese, beer, wine and bread to preserves, ice cream and pies—all made from locally grown ingredients. The natural environment is also a rich food source, providing everything from freshwater fish to succulent berries to wild mushrooms.

Food is a vital part of history and culture. It reflects a place and the people who live there. B.C.'s food producers have a rich history that ties their origins with their present places to create a unique and diverse culture. People from all over the world have settled in B.C. and brought their traditional foods with them. Their recipes have changed and adapted to the locally available resources. We like to say that in B.C. we taste the best ideas from around the world and make them our own using our amazing local ingredients.

In the past, if a food wasn't in season, we probably couldn't get it. The foods we ate changed depending on the time of the year, and we had an intimate connection with our food and where it came from. Now fresh food can quickly travel from around the world to our dinner tables. Wide selection and convenience are the great advantages of our modern world. The great disadvantage is that we have become disconnected from where our food comes from. We give little thought to how far it has had to travel and what financial, ethical or environmental costs the production of imported food may have.

Eating seasonally takes advantage of what locally grown foods are available. It supports the local economy, and it often provides us with fresher and tastier food. Perhaps most importantly, it connects us to the origins of our food. By speaking directly to food producers at such places as farmers' markets, U-pick farms and wineries, we learn not only the bounty of foods available at home, but the value of the people involved in their production. We can even become food producers ourselves, by growing our own fruits or vegetables in our gardens or balcony planters.

With this book, we have created a resource of recipes that represent some of the best of what B.C. has to offer. Meat, fowl, eggs, cheese and wine are available all year and can be combined with seasonal foods that change throughout the year. Spring offers us tender asparagus, buttery spinach and sweet, crisp peas. Summer brings many fresh fruits, wonderful to enjoy in pies, ice cream and smoothies. Fall's first frost sweetens cabbage, broccoli and kale. Winter warming comes in the form of roasted root vegetables and soups. It's all here, in the appetizers, salads, soups, main and side dishes, desserts and snacks that make up the seasons of this book.

About the Authors

Canadian chef Jennifer Ogle learned her craft from a variety of sources, among them the renowned French cooking school *La Varenne,* which lead to an opportunity to work in the Michelin-starred restaurant *La Madeleine* in Burgundy, France.

Eric Pateman, president and founder of Edible British Columbia, has worked in the hospitality industry for over 15 years both as a chef and hotel consultant. Eric's travels have taken him throughout North America, to the United Kingdom and Africa, where he has sought out unique food experiences.

In Our Kitchen

We have found the following ingredient choices and cooking procedures to be successful in our kitchen and recommend them highly wherever possible.

Butter is unsalted and is easiest to measure using the convenient markings on the wrapping.

Citrus juices are fresh squeezed.

Eggs are large, free-run eggs. They should be at room temperature for baking.

Flour is unbleached all-purpose.

Herbs are fresh, unless stated otherwise. In a pinch, the best alternative to fresh is frozen, not dried. You can freeze herbs yourself in the summer when they are plentiful, and you can even find them in the freezer section of some of the better grocery stores.

Mushrooms, such as morels and chanterelles, can be found in the wild, but we advise that you confirm the identification of mushrooms with an experienced collector before cooking them; some species of mushrooms are acutely toxic and can cause death.

Stocks are homemade. Good quality stocks available in tetra packs are the best substitute. Avoid using those nasty little cubes. Miso, a fermented soybean paste, is another interesting alternative to stock, and it will keep in the refrigerator for several months. Stir it in 1 Tbsp (15 mL) at a time until you have a rich, full flavour.

Sugar is organic and unrefined rather than white and bleached. When looking for a rich brown sugar, use muscovado sugar, available in grocery and health food stores. It still contains the minerals and vitamins originally in the sugar cane plant, and it has a full molasses flavour.

Yeast is regular dry yeast; ½ oz (15 g) dry yeast is equal to 1 Tbsp fresh yeast.

Essential Ingredients

The following ingredients are used in many of the recipes in this book; special ingredients found in just one or two recipes are described where they are used. Some items are widely available, whereas others are best sought in gourmet, specialty food, health food or ethnic stores or obtained by mail order or the Internet.

Bay Leaves— Fresh leaves have such a different flavour that they are worth the effort to find. They are occasionally available at large grocery stores and can be specially ordered. In a well-sealed container in the fridge, they can last three or four months.

Coconut Milk—Use unsweetened coconut milk in cans. Naturally sweet, it is often better than cream in savory dishes.

Garlic—Use fresh garlic! An Italian friend once told me that if you can't be bothered to peel and chop fresh garlic you shouldn't be allowed to use it!

Lemons and Limes—Use fresh! You can't compare the taste to concentrate.

Mayonnaise—It's always better homemade:

5 egg yolks

⅔ cup (150 mL) extra virgin olive oil

¼ cup (60 mL) good quality vinegar or juice of 1 lemon

pinch of sea salt to taste

- You need both hands free to make mayonnaise. Spread a damp cloth on your counter, nestle a medium-sized bowl in its centre and wrap it around base of bowl to keep it steady while you whisk.

- Whisk yolk, vinegar and salt in bowl until well combined and yolk has lightened in colour.

- Add oil, a drop at a time, whisking continuously until mixture emulsifies and thickens.

- When about half of oil has been added, add remaining oil in a slow, steady stream. Store, covered, in refrigerator for up to 5 days. You can thin your mayonnaise by lightly whisking in some water.

- Many people like to add mustard or fresh herbs to their mayonnaise. Adding minced garlic turns plain mayonnaise into aioli. Makes just over 1 cup (250 mL).

Mustard—Use good quality mustard for everything from sandwiches to dressings to sauces. When you are down to the last few teaspoons clinging to the bottom of your mustard jar, add fresh lemon juice, olive oil, sea salt and fresh pepper for a yummy impromptu salad dressing. Just shake and enjoy.

Oil, Sesame—Use for a nutty flavour addition. Store it in the fridge.

Oil, Olive—Extra virgin olive oil is indispensable. Try olive oil from Italy, Spain or Greece.

Oil, Grape Seed —Use for higher heat cooking.

Pepper, Fresh—Please don't use pre-ground pepper; it has such poor flavour. A variety of peppercorns are available. Black or white can be used interchangeably in any of the recipes.

Salt—Great salt is the key to great cooking. Salt brings out the flavour in food. Sea salt, kosher salt, Celtic salt—choose a favourite. Better yet, obtain some of each. Using a better quality salt also means that you will use less, because the flavour is more intense. If you need to reduce salt even further for health reasons, use fresh herbs, various spices and flavour lifters, such as lemon juice, to maintain the flavour intensity while reducing the salt content.

Soy Sauce—Both tamari and shoyu are high quality, fermented and chemical-free "soy sauces" that are used to enhance flavour and impart a unique saltiness.

Star Anise—This strongly anise-scented Oriental spice is commonly sold dried, as quarter-sized, star-shaped clusters of 5 to 10 pods, each containing a single seed. The seeds can be used on their own, crushed or ground, or the entire stars can be added, then removed.

Vinegar, Apple Cider—Use when you need an all-purpose vinegar; organic, unrefined and unpasteurized has the best flavour.

Vinegar, Balsamic—Its unique flavour is great in everything from soups to sweets. Be sure to try B.C.'s own balsamic such as Venturi Schulze of Okanagan Vinegar Brewery.

Measuring

Dry ingredients should be spooned into the measuring cup and leveled off with a knife or spatula.

Measurements are in both metric and imperial. Note that for butter, a pound is considered to be 454 g; for meat, vegetables, etc., a pound is 500 g.

Solids, including butter and most cheeses, are measured in dry-measure cups and liquids in liquid-measure cups.

Spring Heirloom Tomato Salad

Serves 4

If you are interested in tomatoes—those tomatoes reminiscent of days in the garden as a child picking the sun-warmed fruit right off the vine—then look no further than Stoney Paradise Tomatoes and Milan Djordjevich. In past years Milan could be found at the Granville Island Farmers' Market. Be sure to call Stoney Paradise to find out where to find his tomatoes this summer!

1 clove garlic, minced

splash of white balsamic vinegar (see Essential Ingredients, p. 6)

¼ cup (60 mL) olive oil

sea salt and freshly ground pepper to taste

1 lb (500 g) heirloom tomatoes, washed, cored and sliced ½ in (1 cm) thick

½ lb (250 g) bocconcini, sliced the same thickness as the tomatoes

handful of fresh basil leaves, washed and patted dry

French baguette

In a salad bowl, add the garlic, vinegar and oil. Then add the tomatoes, tossing gently to coat with dressing. Season to taste with salt and pepper.

On individual plates, layer tomato slices with bocconcini and some basil tucked in between and around the tomato slices. Scatter remaining basil leaves on top and drizzle remaining dressing.

Serve with slices of crusty French baguette.

Tip
Fresh tomatoes from the garden or the farmers' market would also work in this recipe.

Bocconcini are a form of semi-ripe mozzarella cheese that comes in small, soft, white balls.

Asparagus and Carmelis Chèvre Salad

Serves 4

B.C., like other Canadian provinces, is dotted with artisan goat cheese producers. One to visit if you are in the Okanagan is nestled on a hillside outside of
Kelowna overlooking the lake. Carmelis is a family-owned boutique dairy that
produces a multitude of delicious goat cheeses for all tastes with milk from goats
raised on their farm. One of their most popular styles of cheese is *chèvre* (French
for "goat"), a tangy fluffy and soft cheese synonymous with the French style of
goat cheese.

**1 x 2 lbs (1 kg) bunch of
asparagus, trimmed**

splash of olive oil

**sea salt and freshly ground
pepper to taste**

**1 lb (500 g) package frozen
peas, refreshed in boiling
water, drained and cooled**

**1 cup (250 g) chèvre,
crumbled**

**½ cup (125 mL) fresh mint,
chopped**

**½ cup (125 mL) fresh basil,
chopped**

1 lime cut into 4 wedges

Preheat barbecue to medium-high heat. Toss
trimmed asparagus with olive oil, salt and pepper.
Grill for 4 minutes, turning once. Set aside.

In a bowl, toss together the remaining ingredients, except the lime. Cut the warm asparagus
into bite-sized pieces and add to the bowl, toss
and season again if needed. (You cut the asparagus after because it is much easier to grill if left
whole!) Divide among 4 plates and garnish each
salad with a lime wedge.

Tip
Soft cheeses such as chèvre
do not slice well—they often end
up as a crumbled mess, half stuck
to the knife. The easiest way to cut
soft cheese is with taut dental floss.
Just be sure to use unflavoured floss!

Tip
Allow cheese to come to room temperature for at least 30 minutes (longer for hard cheese or if the room is particularly cold) before serving in order to enjoy its full flavour and aroma. Portion cheese, if desired, while cold and keep it wrapped so it doesn't dry out before you are ready to serve.

Fresh Pea and Mint Pasta Salad

Serves 4 to 6

Fresh peas are a hallmark of early summer in southwestern British Columbia and are a favourite crop among backyard gardeners and commercial growers alike. B.C. produces more than 9900 tons (9000 tonnes) of peas each year, 90% of which are shelled and processed; however, on the home front, fresh green peas that are shelled at the sink are more likely to be eaten on the spot than make it to the table! A cool-climate crop, peas come into season in June and are available fresh at local farmers' markets, U-pick farms, produce merchants and many grocery stores. B.C. (and Western Washington) produce the highest quality and highest yielding peas in all of North America.

1 x 12 oz (340 g) package pasta, cooked and cooled (see Tip)

1 cup (250 mL) cherry tomatoes, halved

½ small red onion, halved and very thinly sliced

2 cups (500 mL) fresh peas

2 Tbsp (30 mL) fresh mint, finely chopped

1 Tbsp (15 mL) fresh oregano, finely chopped

1 cup (250 mL) chopped roasted chicken (optional)

In a large bowl, gently toss the pasta, tomatoes, onion, peas, mint, oregano and chicken, if using. In a small bowl, whisk the dressing ingredients together, pour over the salad and toss again. Serve immediately, or store, covered, in the refrigerator until ready to serve as a side dish.

Tip
Pastas such as gemelli, fusilli, rotini or radiatore are perfect for pasta salads because their texture holds the dressing nicely.

Peas are a legume and, like most legumes, have special nodules on their roots that enable them to take nitrogen from the air and return it to the soil. This function actually allows the peas to enrich the soil they grow in.

Dressing

2 Tbsp (30 mL) white wine vinegar

¼ cup (60 mL) olive oil

½ tsp (2 mL) Dijon mustard

3 Tbsp (45 mL) mayonnaise

sea salt and freshly ground pepper to taste

Cipollini and Asiago Stuffed Morels

Serves 4 as an appetizer

The morel is a species of mushroom highly coveted by B.C. chefs. Known for their nut-like flavour and meaty texture, morels grow year after year on the same forested sites, preferring the company of ash trees, but they flourish in the years immediately following a forest fire. Since the Okanagan forest fire of 2003, the Okanagan Valley (along with other fire-prone regions of B.C.) has seen a bumper crop of these tasty jewels of the forest. When stuffed with sweet cipollini onions and salty Italian cheese, these mushrooms make a perfect appetizer.

1 Tbsp (15 mL) grape seed or canola oil

½ cup (125 mL) cipollini onion, peeled and quartered

1 lb (500 g) fresh morels; reserve 12 of the largest ones to stuff and chop the rest for stuffing

¼ cup (60 mL) white wine

1 clove garlic, minced

¼ cup (60 mL) parsley, chopped

2 Tbsp (30 mL) chives, chopped

¼ cup (60 mL) grated Asiago cheese

2 to 3 Tbsp (30 to 45 mL) panko (see p. 57)

sea salt and freshly ground pepper to taste

In a medium saucepan, heat the oil over medium heat and sauté the cipollini onions until they start to caramelize, about 5 minutes. Add the chopped mushrooms, white wine and cook for about 5 minutes. Add garlic, cook for 2 to 3 minutes and remove pan from heat. Stir in remaining ingredients, except for the 12 reserved morels. Stuff the reserved mushrooms with the filling.

For the lime mayonnaise, stir together lime zest and mayonnaise. Set aside.

For breading, place flour, eggs and panko into separate bowls. Heat clarified butter in a saucepan over medium-high heat. Bread the stuffed morels one at a time, dipping first in the flour, then the egg and finally the panko. Cook the mushrooms in the butter until brown and crispy. Serve hot with lime mayonnaise.

Tip
To remove any unwanted critters hiding in the morels, soak mushrooms in salted water for at least 1 hour.

Tip
To make clarified butter, melt unsalted butter slowly over low heat. Gradually, froth will rise to the top with a layer of clear golden oil in the middle and a layer of milk solids on the bottom. Clarified butter is the middle layer. Skim off the froth and carefully ladle out the clear oil, leaving out the milk solids.

Lime Mayonnaise
zest from 1 lime
½ cup (125 mL) mayonnaise
(see Essential Ingredients, p. 6)

Breading
½ cup (125 mL) flour
3 eggs, lightly beaten
2 cups (500 mL) panko
1 cup (250 mL) clarified butter (see Tip)

Wild Mushroom Soup with Parsley Froth

Serves 6

Foraging for mushrooms is a pleasant and secretive pastime for many B.C. residents. The locations of the "best spots" for mushroom hunting are rarely disclosed and are spoken of in hushed tones, even within the family. Historically, the pine mushroom is the only species known to have been traditionally eaten by the First Nations of B.C., and only by the Nlaka'pamux (Thompson River) and Stl'atl'imx (Lillooet) peoples. In the early 20th century, Japanese immigrants began to collect the pine mushroom (matsutake) for consumption and for sale. Today, the prized selections for both commercial and home foragers include morels, chanterelles, lobster and pine mushrooms and B.C.'s multimillion dollar wild-mushroom industry ships to mushroom lovers all over the world.

3 cups (750 mL) fresh, cleaned wild mushrooms, such as chanterelles, lobster or morels

2 Tbsp (30 mL) olive oil

¼ cup (60 mL) unsalted butter

1 large yellow onion, diced

2 large Yukon Gold potatoes, diced

¼ cup (60 mL) dry sherry

1 bouquet garni of parsley, thyme and bay leaf

3 dried juniper berries, bruised

4 cloves garlic, minced

8 cups (2 L) chicken or vegetable stock

1 cup (250 mL) heavy cream (32%)

Slice mushrooms into even-sized pieces and sauté in batches in a large pot with olive oil and half of butter until nicely browned. Remove mushrooms and set aside. In same pot, melt remaining butter and add onions and potatoes. Sauté until golden, then deglaze with sherry. Add bouquet garni, juniper berries, garlic, sautéed mushrooms and stock. Bring to a boil, then immediately reduce heat to a simmer and cook until liquid has reduced by one-third.

Add cream, bring almost to a boil and remove from heat. Remove bouquet garni. Purée soup in a blender until smooth. Serve hot, garnished with parsley froth (see opposite).

Parsley Froth

Blanch parsley, drain and squeeze dry. Purée parsley and pass through a fine mesh strainer. Scald milk in a pot, remove from heat and add parsley. Just before serving, blend with an immersion (stick) blender until frothy.

1 cup (250 mL) fresh parsley, chopped

1 cup (250 mL) milk

Tip

If suitable fresh wild mushrooms are not available, you can use half the quantity of dried wild mushrooms. Reconstitute them in hot water or stock for about 10 minutes. Add enough liquid to cover, using a small plate to keep them submerged. Save the liquid to add to your soup; it will be full of great mushroom flavour.

Warning

Because some mushrooms contain deadly toxins, eat only mushrooms positively identified as edible.

Salt Spring Island Lamb with Mustard Spaetzle

Serves 4

So renowned is the taste and texture of Salt Spring Island lamb that many visitors to British Columbia ask for it by name. Even HRH Queen Elizabeth is said to prefer it to lamb from any other corner of her Commonwealth. What makes Gulf Island lamb so unique? Perhaps it is the salt water from the ocean that travels inland on the wind to settle on the grass where the sheep graze. Or the rich, grainy diet the sheep and lambs are fed. It could just be the laid back island lifestyle into which the lambs are born. Luckily for us locals, the lamb is available at Granville Island and through other top-quality butchers and restaurateurs.

2 x 1½ lbs (750 g) lamb racks, frenched (trimmed and ready to use; available in most grocery stores)

2 Tbsp (30 mL) extra virgin olive oil

sea salt and freshly ground pepper

1 clove garlic, minced

1 cup (250 mL) fresh parsley, chopped

2 Tbsp (30 mL) each fresh thyme and rosemary, chopped

¼ cup (60 mL) breadcrumbs

¼ cup (60 mL) Dijon mustard

Spaetzle
1¼ cups (310 mL) flour

1 tsp (5 mL) sea salt

3 large eggs

⅓ cup (75 mL) milk

1 Tbsp (15 mL) grainy Dijon mustard

Place a heavy-bottomed pan over medium-high heat. Brush lamb with oil and season with salt and pepper. Sear lamb until brown on all sides. Remove from heat and let sit 15 minutes.

Preheat oven to 450° F (230° C). Mix garlic and herbs together in a bowl with breadcrumbs. Place lamb on a small, rimmed baking sheet; brush Dijon mustard on rounded side of lamb. Divide breadcrumb mixture evenly over chops, covering mustard to form a crust. Bake for 10 to 15 minutes or until a thermometer inserted in centre reaches 140° F (60° C) for medium rare. Let rest 5 to 10 minutes before cutting into chops. Serve with spaetzle (below).

Bring a large pot of salted water to a boil. Set a bowl of ice water near pot. Sift flour and salt together. Whisk together eggs, milk and Dijon mustard and pour into flour, stirring to make a smooth batter. Using a spaetzle maker or food mill, drop batter into boiling water. When spaetzle come to surface, transfer them to ice water with a slotted spoon. Repeat until all batter is used. As they cool, remove spaetzle from water and place in sieve to drain. To reheat spaetzle, toss them in hot butter or sauce—or fry them over medium heat until golden.

Spaetzle or spätzle ("little sparrow") are German dumplings very similar to pasta. They are served as a side dish and are common fare, especially in southern Germany and the Alsace region. Spaetzle makers are available at specialty food shops, department stores and German markets (where you will likely find a good one for a reasonable price).

Tuna Carpaccio

Serves 6 to 8

Albacore tuna caught in the waters off of British Columbia's west coast is available fresh from late June through early fall. Its increasing popularity on the fresh sheet at local fishmongers is largely a result of our love affair with Japanese sushi. B.C.'s albacore is fished in a sustainable manner, which avoids possible bycatch problems and yields lower mercury levels, thus meeting the Vancouver Aquarium Ocean Wise program criteria honoured by many top restaurateurs. This recipe showcases albacore tuna's fresh, mild flavour and succulent texture. Be sure to use sashimi grade fish from a reliable fishmonger.

1 x 3 to 4 lbs (1.5. kg to 2 kg) sashimi-quality tuna loin, skinned and trimmed of any sinew

¼ cup (60 mL) fresh thyme, very finely chopped

¼ cup (60 mL) fresh mint, very finely chopped

1 long green chili, such as jalepeño or serrano, seeded and finely chopped

grated zest and juice of 1 lime

1 Tbsp (15 mL) rice wine vinegar

¼ cup (60 mL) sesame oil

4 lime wedges

Roll the tuna loin in the thyme and mint, ensuring it is completely coated. Wrap tightly in plastic wrap and refrigerate for 2 hours.

Combine chili, lime zest and juice, rice wine vinegar and sesame oil to make the dressing.

When ready to serve, unwrap the tuna and cut into paper-thin slices with a very sharp knife. Drizzle dressing over slices of tuna on serving plates with mesclun and lime wedges on the side.

Tip

It is easier to slice tuna into paper-thin slices when it is partially frozen. Try using frozen sashimi-quality tuna, thaw it slightly to coat with herbs and then refreeze before slicing.

Smoked Salmon with Asparagus Salad

Serves 4

This incredibly delicious salad offers the opportunity to use many amazing B.C. products, including fresh asparagus, cranberries, honey and most importantly—smoked salmon! This delicacy of the West Coast is generally on the top of the list of items visitors like to take back home with them. This recipe uses cold smoked salmon, or lox, as it is sometimes called, which is salmon that is cured but not cooked, so it has a unique flavour and texture. Smoked salmon is available as hot smoked, jerky, Indian candy or even as Tandoori nuggets. Be sure to try one of these products the next time you are at your local fish counter.

¹/₄ cup (60 mL) dried sweetened cranberries, coarsely chopped

1 Tbsp (15 mL) capers, drained and chopped

2 tsp (10 mL) honey

2 tsp (10 mL) balsamic vinegar

1 garlic clove, minced

2 Tbsp (30 mL) olive oil

sea salt and freshly ground pepper

1 x 2 lbs (1 kg) bunch of asparagus, trimmed

5 oz (150 g) cold smoked salmon slices

¹/₃ cup (75 mL) crème fraîche (see Tip)

1 large, ripe avocado, sliced

chives and dill for garnish

Combine cranberries, capers, honey, vinegar, garlic, oil and salt and pepper in a small saucepan. Stir over medium heat until warm. Let stand for 15 minutes to allow the cranberries to soften.

Blanch asparagus in a large saucepan of boiling, salted water for about 2 minutes or until bright green; drain. Immediately place asparagus in a bowl of iced water. Let stand about 10 minutes or until cool; drain. Return asparagus to same bowl. Add cranberry dressing and toss to combine.

Arrange asparagus on 4 serving plates; drizzle with dressing. Top with smoked salmon, some crème fraîche, avocado, more crème fraîche and smoked salmon. Garnish with chives and dill if desired.

Tip
If crème fraîche isn't available, you can substitute with sour cream.

Spring, coho and sockeye salmon, with their higher fat content, have the best flavour when smoked.

Gnocchi in a Sorrel Sauce

Serves 2 as a main course, 4 as a side dish

Gnocchi, which means "dumplings" in Italian, are one of the most versatile Italian dishes. Commonly made using potato and semolina flour, these little balls should be as light as air. They work well with a variety of sauces, including this tasty sorrel sauce. But also try variations, including creamy blue cheese, truffles or even just a simple meat sauce. The secret to gnocchi is not to overcook them because they will start to fall apart. As with all Italian pasta dishes, al dente, or "tender to the tooth," is the desired doneness!

1 lb (500 g) package gnocchi

splash of olive oil

1 Tbsp (15 mL) unsalted butter

1 small shallot, minced

½ cup (125 mL) white wine

1 cup (250 mL) heavy cream (32%)

1 packed cup (250 g) sorrel, chopped

¼ cup (60 mL) parsley, chopped

sea salt and freshly ground pepper to taste

good sized pinch of fresh chives, chopped

handful of fresh grated Parmesan cheese

Bring a big pot of salted water to a rolling boil and cook the gnocchi until they float to the surface. Drain, toss with a splash of olive oil and set aside.

In a large saucepan, heat the butter and add the shallot and cook for 2 to 3 minutes, then add the white wine and cook until the wine has reduced by half. Add the cream and continue cooking for 5 minutes at medium-high heat.

Purée sorrel and parsley in a blender along with hot cream mixture until everything is incorporated; the sauce turns a jade green colour. Pour sauce back into pan along with the gnocchi just to heat through and season with salt and pepper. Serve in warm bowls with chives and Parmesan cheese sprinkled on top.

Gnocchi are often made using potatoes, but they can also be made with durum wheat, flour or ricotta cheese. Traditionally, gnocchi are served with tomato sauce or melted butter and Parmesan cheese, but they lend themselves well to almost any sauce.

Herb Pesto

Makes about 2 cups (500 mL)

Basil thrives in the heat of summer, and it will grow in abundance if it is kept in a humid environment. It does not tolerate cold weather, so when growing basil in B.C., be sure there is no chance of frost. It can also be planted indoors, preferably in a south-facing window. Basil is thought to have originated in India, where it was considered a holy plant and often planted near shrines and temples. Legend has it that the Greeks named the plant βασιλευς, meaning "king," when it was found growing above the spot where the Holy Cross was rediscovered in the 4th century AD. Even today, basil is considered the high priest of herbs. There are dozens of varieties available, from licorice basil and cinnamon-flavoured basil to purple varieties and spicy warm ones, such as Thai basil.

4 cups (32 oz) fresh basil leaves, rinsed, patted dry and well packed

4 cloves garlic, peeled

1 cup (250 mL) pine nuts or other nut of your choice

1½ cups (375 mL) freshly grated Parmesan or Pecorino cheese

1½ cups (375 mL) extra virgin olive oil

sea salt and freshly ground pepper to taste

In a blender, pulse basil and garlic until well crushed. Add nuts, process to crush, then add cheese. You should have a thick paste. Slowly drizzle in olive oil, continuously mixing. Adjust seasoning and serve with pasta or vegetables, or add to a soup, etc.

Tip
Traditionally, pesto is made in a mortar and pestle. A food processor also works just fine—the method is the same.

Variation
Genoa, Italy, is the birthplace of pesto, where it is traditionally made with basil and pine nuts. For variety, try other herbs, such as arugula, cilantro or even cooked artichokes, or nuts and seeds, such as walnuts and sunflower kernels.

Potato Frittata

Serves 4

Potatoes are a popular kitchen staple because they are cheap, easy to cook and tasty, making them a comfort food that adapts well to many recipes. B.C. produces more than 78,000 tons (71,000 tonnes) of potatoes each year, valued at more than $20 million! Amazingly, the average Canadian eats about 163 pounds (74 kilograms) of potatoes per year. Derived from the Italian word *fritto* ("fried"), a frittata is an open-faced omelette made with cheese and other ingredients mixed into the eggs. It is a classic Roman dish traditionally served on Easter Day. Incorporating potatoes into this breakfast dish makes it an especially satisfying and comforting one-dish meal.

2 Tbsp (30 mL) butter

3 onions, sliced

2 medium Yukon Gold potatoes, peeled, cooked and sliced

8 eggs

¾ cup (175 mL) cream or milk

sea salt and freshly ground black pepper

½ cup (125 mL) aged Cheddar cheese, grated

1 Tbsp (15 mL) fresh thyme, chopped

Preheat broiler to 500° F (260° C). Melt butter in a 9-inch (23 cm) nonstick, ovenproof pan over low heat. Add onions and sauté, stirring occasionally, for 10 to 15 minutes until onions are golden brown. Add potato slices and cook until starting to brown, about 5 minutes. Whisk eggs, cream or milk, salt and pepper in a bowl to combine. Pour egg mixture over onions in frying pan and sprinkle with cheese and thyme. Cook frittata for 5 to 6 minutes or until it is almost set. To finish cooking, place frittata under broiler for 1 minute. Cut into wedges and serve along with your breakfast favourites.

Potatoes are the most widely grown vegetable in the world.
In B.C., more potatoes are grown than any other vegetable.

Braised Swiss Chard

Serves 4

With its bright red stalks and dark green leaves, this cool-climate lover is an ideal B.C. vegetable because it can withstand frost, and when planted in early spring, it is usually ready to eat within four to six weeks. It also rivals spinach as a great leafy green because, unlike spinach, it contains no oxalic acid, so the minerals it contains are more readily digestible. Chard is a kind of beet grown for its leaves rather than its roots. It packs a huge amount of vitamin A and is naturally high in sodium—one cup (250 ml) contains 313 mg. This is the perfect spring vegetable because the tips are very tender and it offers a much different taste at this time of the year than in the fall, when it is typically consumed. Try also using it raw in a salad!

2 small red onions, chopped

1 Tbsp (15 mL) butter

2 lbs (1 kg) chard leaves, stems removed

¼ cup (60 mL) white wine

sea salt and freshly ground pepper to taste

Sauté the onions in the butter over medium heat in a large pan until they are nearly softened and lightly browned, about 8 to 10 minutes. Meanwhile, clean chard leaves (see Tip) and slice into ribbons.

Add the chard leaves and wine. Cook rapidly, stirring frequently, until the chard is wilted and the liquid has evaporated, about 5 minutes.

Season with salt and pepper, and serve as a side dish.

Tip
To clean chard, simply swish in cool water and pat dry. The stems and leaves are both edible, but should be cooked separately because the stems take longer to cook.

Chard can be used instead of spinach or kale in your favourite recipes.

Apple Cranberry Cinnamon Buns

Makes 12

Cinnamon rolls are a North American and Northern European tradition, with entire stores in malls now dedicated to selling these sweet, sticky pastries. However, the best cinnamon rolls are the ones that come straight out of your oven, filling the house with the incomparable homeyness of baked bread and cinnamon. This variation of the traditional roll incorporates two of B.C.'s best known fruits: Granny Smith apples and Fraser Valley cranberries. Their tartness will counter all the sugar and icing plus lend a local flavour. Served warm on a Sunday morning, these make the perfect weekend brunch treat.

Dough

¼ cup (60 mL) warm water

1 Tbsp (15 mL) active dry yeast

¼ cup (60 mL) sugar

2¼ cups (560 mL) flour

½ cup (125 mL) buttermilk at room temperature

1 tsp (5 mL) salt

2 large egg yolks

¼ cup (60 mL) unsalted butter, softened

Filling

½ cup (125 mL) dried cranberries

2 Granny Smith apples, peeled and chopped

⅓ cup (75 mL) brown sugar

1 tsp (5 mL) cinnamon

1 tsp (5 mL) cardamom

2 Tbsp (30 mL) unsalted butter, melted and cooled slightly

Sprinkle yeast over warm water with 1 tsp (5 mL) sugar and let stand until foamy, 5 to 10 minutes. Add remaining sugar, flour, buttermilk, salt and yolks, and stir until everything is combined well. Transfer mixture to an electric mixer with a dough hook and beat in butter, a few pieces at a time, on medium speed until smooth and elastic, about 5 minutes. Scrape dough from side of bowl and cover bowl with plastic wrap in a warm place for 1 hour or until dough has doubled in size.

In a small bowl, stir together cranberries with the apples. In another bowl, stir together sugar, cinnamon and cardamom.

Grease a 9 x 13 inch (23 x 33 cm) baking pan. Transfer dough onto a floured surface and roll out into a 16 x 12 inch (40 x 30 cm) rectangle. Brush dough with melted butter, leaving an unbuttered ½-inch (1 cm) border on long sides. Sprinkle fruit filling evenly over the buttered area and then sprinkle cinnamon-cardamom sugar evenly over the filling. Roll up the shorter side of the dough, like a jelly roll, and pinch to seal the edge firmly. Cut into 12 even pieces and arrange, cut sides down, in the baking pan. Cover loosely with plastic wrap and let the buns rise in a warm place for 45 to 50 minutes or until they have doubled in size.

While buns are rising, preheat oven to 350° F (175° C). Bake buns in middle of oven until golden, about 25 minutes. Transfer buns to a rack and cool slightly before serving.

Since 1999, Sweden has celebrated National Cinnamon Bun Day on October 4 each year.

Asparagus Omelette

Serves 1

A sure sign of spring is the arrival of local asparagus on the shelves at our many green grocers. This unique vegetable takes more than three years from its initial planting to actually start producing the tender shoots that are suitable for harvest. Some farms in B.C. also produce white asparagus, which is similar to the green variety, but instead of letting the shoots come out of the ground, the farmer keeps covering the stalks with more dirt as they grow, shielding them from the light. By doing this, the stalks never develop any colour and are then harvested as white asparagus.

3 eggs, separated

2 Tbsp (30 mL) cream (10 to 18 %)

1 Tbsp (15 mL) unsalted butter

pinch of sea salt and freshly ground pepper

6 thin asparagus stalks, or 3 thick, lightly steamed

2 Tbsp (30 mL) Salt Spring Island Chévre

1 Tbsp (15 mL) fresh chopped chives

In a medium bowl, blend egg yolks and cream with a fork. In another bowl, beat the whites until soft peaks form. Gently fold the whites into the yolks. In a nonstick 10-inch (25 cm) pan, melt butter over medium-high heat. Pour in eggs, swirling around pan to distribute evenly. Season with salt and pepper. Using a spatula, push the eggs gently around to allow the uncooked egg to flow underneath, running the spatula around the sides of the omelette to loosen. When the eggs are almost set, about 40 seconds, lay the asparagus and cheese in the middle of the omelette. Fold one-third of the omelette over the filling, then lift the pan and slide the opposite third onto your plate and fold the omelette onto itself, forming a neat tri-fold package. Sprinkle with chives and serve immediately.

Tip
When buying asparagus, choose firm, bright green stalks for the best flavour.

Ruth's Unbaked Strawberry Cheesecake

Serves 8

The first strawberries of the season are generally ready for harvest sometime in June and are one of the first fruits each season that signify the start of summer. In B.C., we grow over 6 million pounds (2.7 million kilograms) of strawberries a year, which is more than a quarter of Canada's total production. The bulk of these come from the Fraser Valley, where many U-pick farms feature strawberries and attract a loyal following each year. For the do-it-yourself type of person, strawberries are easy to grow in a container garden on your deck or balcony. This recipe is an unbaked cheesecake, which we find creamier and not as heavy as baked cheesecakes, and it's more suited to the juicy strawberries.

Crust
2 cups (500 mL) graham wafer crumbs

½ cup (125 mL) + 1 Tbsp (15 mL) unsalted butter, melted

zest of 1 lemon, finely chopped

Filling
3 x 250 g (8 oz) packages cream cheese, at room temperature

½ to 1 cup (125 to 250 mL) icing sugar, sifted

fresh lemon juice

⅓ cup (75 mL) whipping cream (32%)

Topping
1 x 8 oz (250 mL) jar of apple jelly

1 lb (500 g) strawberries, whole, washed and stemmed

Preheat oven to 350° F (175° C). Crush graham wafers with a rolling pin or pulse in a food processor to make crumbs. In a mixing bowl, combine the graham wafer crumbs, melted butter and lemon zest. Pat the mixture evenly into a 10-inch (25 cm) pie plate. Bake in the oven for 10 minutes. Cool to room temperature. Cover and chill in the refrigerator until ready to fill. Crust can be made a day in advance.

In a food processor, combine cream cheese, icing sugar and a generous squeeze of lemon juice. Mix until smooth and creamy. Transfer into a large mixing bowl.

In a small bowl, beat the whipping cream until light and fluffy, and fold into the cream cheese mixture. Gently fill the chilled graham crust with the creamy filling and chill for at least 3 hours before serving.

To prepare the topping, gently heat the apple jelly until just warm in a small saucepan. In a medium bowl, pour the warm jelly over the strawberries and mix lightly. Arrange the glazed strawberries on top of the cheesecake.

Tip
You can use the bottom of a small glass to help press the graham wafer crumbs evenly on the pie plate.

Rhubarb Pie with a Meringue Crust

Serves 6

Rhubarb is one of those things you either love or hate—there doesn't ever seem to be any middle ground on the subject. For early pioneers, the robust and hardy rhubarb plant supplied essential vitamins and minerals in spring before any berries ripened. Indigenous to Asia, rhubarb was first brought to Europe for its medicinal qualities. Huge plantations were soon established in Oxfordshire and Bedfordshire, England, where they still grow today. Officially recognized in Europe as a food, rhubarb was known as "pie plant" because it was most often presented as a pie filling and in other desserts. It was also the English who brought the first rhubarb to Canada. This recipe offers a nice balance between the tart rhubarb and the sweet meringue crust. And remember, don't eat the plant's leaves—they're poisonous.

1 cup (250 mL) sugar

3 Tbsp (45 mL) flour

1 tsp (5 mL) cinnamon

2 lbs (1 kg) rhubarb, frozen or fresh

1 x 9-inch (23 cm) pie crust, prebaked (or see p. 81 for Great Pie Crust)

Meringue

⅓ cup (75 mL) sugar

1 Tbsp (15 mL) cornstarch

5 egg whites

½ tsp (2 mL) cream of tartar

Mix together sugar, flour and cinnamon in a large bowl. Slice rhubarb into 1-inch (2.5 cm) pieces, add to the flour-sugar mixture and mix until well coated.

In a saucepan over medium heat, cook rhubarb until it is soft and thickened, about 10 minutes. Let cool for at least 30 minutes.

For the meringue, mix sugar and cornstarch in a small bowl. In another bowl, with an electric mixer, beat egg whites until foamy. Add cream of tartar and beat in sugar-cornstarch mixture, 1 Tbsp (15 mL) at a time, until egg whites are stiff and glossy.

Pour the cooled rhubarb filling into prepared pie crust and spoon meringue gently on top.

Bake the meringue-topped pie at 350° F (175° C) for 10 to 12 minutes, until the meringue is slightly golden.

A member of the buckwheat family, rhubarb is closely related to sorrel. Although rhubarb is technically a vegetable, the stems are used as a fruit in most recipes.

Gazpacho with Fresh Tomato Water

Serves 8

Gazpacho is a cold soup with origins in Spain. It is typically served during the warm summer months using a combination of ingredients, including stale bread, garlic, olive oil, salt and vinegar. It wasn't until the early 16th century that the tomato and bell pepper were introduced to the ingredient list. During the months of July and August in B.C., heirloom tomatoes come into season from specialty growers such as Vista D'Oro Farm in Langley and Stoney Paradise Farm in Kelowna. These tomatoes are as sweet as candy and they create a soup that is beyond compare, as if the flavour of the summer sun were caught in your bowl.

8 ripe tomatoes, peeled, seeded and finely chopped

1 small red onion, finely chopped

1 medium English cucumber, peeled, seeded and finely chopped

1 red pepper, finely chopped

¼ cup (60 mL) fresh parsley, chopped

¼ cup (60 mL) fresh chives, chopped

1 clove garlic, minced

¼ cup (60 mL) red wine vinegar

¼ cup (60 mL) olive oil

juice from ½ or 1 lemon

2 tsp (10 mL) sugar

sea salt and freshly ground pepper to taste

6 or more drops of Tabasco sauce

4 cups (1 L) tomato water

Combine all ingredients. Cover tightly and refrigerate overnight for the best flavour. Serve gazpacho cold with some crusty fresh ciabatta bread.

Tomato Water

Roughly chop 2 lbs (1 kg) ripe tomatoes and mix with 1 Tbsp (15 mL) salt. Line a fine sieve with dampened cheesecloth and set over a large bowl. Pour the tomatoes into the sieve, making sure that the cheesecloth is tied securely, and let the tomatoes sit for at least 12 hours for all the tomato water to drain into the bowl.

Okanagan Apple and Quinoa Salad

Serves 6 as a main-course salad

Kelowna Land and Orchard (KLO) Company is one of Canada's largest producing orchards, and it is located only 10 minutes from the city center of Kelowna. With more than 150 acres (61 hectares) planted and an annual production of more than 4 million pounds (1.8 million kilograms) of fruit, KLO produces a good percentage of the apples that B.C. contributes to Canada's yearly harvest. By pairing local apples from a farm such as KLO with quinoa, which is a seed from a plant in the same family as spinach and buckwheat, you can offer your guests an incredibly healthy and tasty salad. Quinoa is available in the grains section of large grocery stores and health food stores across B.C.

juice from 1 lemon

⅓ cup (75 mL) apple cider vinegar

½ cup (125 mL) orange juice

⅓ cup (75 mL) canola or sunflower oil

⅓ cup (75 mL) honey

5 cups (1.25 L) cooked quinoa (see Tip)

2 apples, cored and chopped

1 bell pepper, diced small

1 cup (250 mL) fresh corn kernels

½ cup (125 mL) dried cranberries

½ cup (125 mL) currants

1 small red onion, finely chopped

1 cup (250 mL) toasted, chopped pecans

1 cup (250 mL) fresh parsley and mint, chopped

sea salt and freshly ground pepper to taste

Place lemon juice, apple cider vinegar, orange juice, oil and honey in a small bowl and stir to combine. In a large bowl, combine quinoa and all remaining ingredients well, then stir in dressing. Adjust seasonings and refrigerate until ready to serve.

Tip

To cook quinoa, bring 4 cups (1 L) water to a boil in a wide-bottomed pot with a lid. Add a pinch of salt and stir in 2 cups (500 mL) quinoa. Reduce heat to a simmer, cover and cook until all the water is absorbed, about 25 minutes. You can cook any amount of quinoa you like as long as you keep the 2:1 ratio of liquid to grain. It is also worth experimenting with other liquids such as stock or coconut milk.

Tip

If there is any leftover quinoa, you can warm it up and add a little cinnamon and cream for a nice breakfast.

Tomato Salad with Bocconcini Tempura

Serves 4

On Vancouver Island, just outside the community of Duncan, lies one of the province's best kept culinary treasures. Fairburn Farm Culinary Retreat and Guesthouse is operated by Chef Mara Jernigan, who is one of our most passionate advocates of slow food and eating local. The farm is also home to Canada's only herd of water buffalo; property owners Darrel and Anthea Archer have started milking them and are now creating Canada's first traditional buffalo mozzarella— perfect for this recipe. You just have to make the trip to the Island to get it!

peanut oil

1 lb (500 g) assorted heirloom tomatoes, sliced into thick rounds

handful of fresh basil

17 oz (500 ml) container mini bocconcini, drained and patted very dry

1 recipe of tempura batter (see p. 142)

extra virgin olive oil or cold-pressed canola oil

juice of 1 lemon

sea salt and freshly ground pepper

Heat peanut oil in pot or deep fryer to 375° F (190° C). Arrange sliced tomato and basil onto individual plates. Dip bocconcini into tempura batter and fry until golden. Serve tempura bocconcini together with tomato slices, drizzle with canola oil and lemon juice. Season with salt and pepper.

Tip

For deep-frying, peanut oil should be 2 to 3 inches (5 to 7.5 cm) deep in pot or use deep fryer according to the manufacturer's directions.

Sweet Corn Bisque

Serves 6

Summer days are long and hot in August, and for many B.C. families, they are the perfect time to hit the road and head to the Fraser Valley or up to the Shuswap. Summer is also corn season, and people year after year return to their favourite stands with claims that they have found the sweetest corn in the province. For those who are city-bound, fresh-picked corn is trucked in and appears at farmers' markets, where people will line up for a taste of summer. Although nothing is as good as corn eaten off the cob, this bisque is a refined way to enjoy the sweetness created by the summer sun.

8 cups (2 L) corn kernels, fresh from the cob or frozen; reserve 2 cups (500 mL) for garnish

¼ cup (60 mL) butter, plus 1 Tbsp (15 mL)

sea salt and freshly ground pepper to taste

2 cups (500 mL) chopped yellow onion

1 clove garlic, minced

3 stalks celery, diced

2 medium carrots, diced

2 sprigs fresh thyme, minced

6 cups (1.5 L) stock

1 cup (250 mL) heavy cream (32%)

tarragon sprigs and thinly sliced red pepper for garnish

Tabasco to taste

In a pot, sauté reserved corn in 1 Tbsp (15 mL) of butter until cooked, about 5 minutes. Season with salt and pepper and set aside. In same pot, sauté onions in ¼ cup (60 mL) of butter until translucent. Add garlic, celery and carrots and sauté for 5 minutes. Add remaining corn and thyme, cover with stock and simmer for 20 minutes. Purée in batches in blender to make a smooth soup and return to heat. Stir in cream, and season with salt, pepper and Tabasco. Garnish each bowl with reserved corn, tarragon and red pepper. Serve hot.

Corn Bread

Preheat oven to 400° F (200° C). Sift together flour, baking powder and salt. Stir in cornmeal. In a separate bowl, cream butter and sugar together, then beat in eggs, one at a time. Stir in buttermilk, then lightly fold wet and dry mixtures together, being sure not to over mix. Bake in two buttered 1-pound (1L) loaf pans for 30 to 35 minutes or until tester comes out clean.

2 cups (500 mL) flour

1 Tbsp (15 mL) baking powder

1 tsp (5 mL) sea salt

2 cups (500 mL) cornmeal

1¼ cups (310 mL) butter

⅓ cup (75 mL) sugar

3 eggs

2 cups (500 mL) buttermilk

Honey-drizzled Figs with Pecan-crusted Goat Cheese

Serves 6

Bee-keeping in B.C. is a huge industry, not for the sweet honey that the bees produce, but rather for the pollination of flowering crops. In fact, the value of bees to agriculture is worth 10 to 20 times the value of all honey and bee products combined. Bees are crucial to B.C.'s cranberry production, for example, and are "employed" during the spring to pollinate the crops. What is amazing about honey is that its flavour varies depending on the type of flowers visited by the bees that produced it. Experiment with this recipe and try using blackberry, blueberry, mountain wildflower or a multitude of other honeys to drizzle on the figs.

1 x 8 oz (250 g) goat cheese log (chèvre)

1 cup (250 mL) toasted, chopped pecans, plus halves for garnish

1 lb (500 g) baby mixed lettuce

⅓ cup (75 mL) extra virgin olive oil

sea salt and freshly ground pepper

12 fresh figs, any variety

½ cup (125 mL) clover honey

Roll goat cheese log in nuts, and wrap in cellophane. Refrigerate at least ½ hour and up to 6 hours.

Arrange lettuce onto 6 plates and sprinkle lightly with olive oil. Season with salt and pepper. Cut figs into halves and arrange atop greens.

Slice cheese into 6 equal-sized rounds and place next to figs. Drizzle with honey, season lightly again with salt and pepper and serve.

For every pound (half kilogram) of honey produced, bees fly over 31,000 miles (50,000 kilometres), which is more than once around the Earth.

Cedar-Planked Salmon with Orange-Pistachio Crust

Serves 4 to 6

Abundant year-round and easily harvested along spawning routes, salmon are traditionally key resources for West Coast First Nations. Equally abundant and important were the cedar trees on the coast. It made sense for the First Nations people to cook their freshly caught salmon on easily split cedar planks. They filleted the salmon and cooked it skin-side down, secured to the plank with saplings. The plank was then propped at an angle above the fire, thus perfuming the meat with a delicate, smoky flavour. Home cooks can still use this traditional preparation today. Just remember, always use wild salmon and be sure to soak the cedar plank for at least two hours before cooking.

1 cup (250 mL) unsalted, shelled pistachios, chopped

²⁄₃ cup (150 mL) panko (see p. 57)

2 Tbsp (30 mL) olive oil

1 Tbsp (15 mL) fresh dill, chopped

2 tsp (10 mL) Dijon mustard

zest from 1 orange

¼ cup (60 mL) orange juice

4 to 6 (8 oz [250 g]) skin-on salmon fillets, any species

2 cedar planks (see Tip)

sea salt and pepper to taste

Preheat grill to medium-high. Mix pistachios and panko together—it works especially well to pulse them together in a food processor. Place on a plate and set aside.

Mix oil, dill, mustard, zest and orange juice to form a paste. Spread paste evenly on flesh side of each salmon fillet, then dip in pistachio and panko mixture. As they are crusted, lay the fillets skin-side down on prepared planks. Season crust with sea salt and freshly ground pepper. Place planks on grill, close lid and cook 12 to 15 minutes.

Tip
Purchase untreated cedar planks, 1 inch (2.5 cm) thick, 8 inches (20 cm) wide and 12 inches (30 cm) long, from your local lumberyard or gourmet shop or via the Internet. The planks must be soaked in water for a minimum of 2 hours, but 4 to 6 hours is best. Drain and pat dry; brush with oil before using. They can often be cleaned and reused several times.

If not available at your supermarket, get preshelled, unsalted pistachios at a Mediterranean or Middle Eastern food store.

Piquant Cream Dill Sauce

Combine all ingredients together in a bowl. Refrigerate sauce for several hours before you plan to serve the salmon, so the flavours can come together.

Experiment with the crust mixture for this recipe or for use with other fish, chicken or meats. A blend of fresh chopped herbs works especially well, or you can add dried, chopped fruit such as apricots or cranberries. For added crunchiness, substitute cornmeal for some of the breadcrumbs.

1 cup (250 mL) sour cream

3 Tbsp (45 mL) mayonnaise

¼ cup (60 mL) fresh dill, finely chopped

1 to 2 Tbsp (15 to 30 mL) drained capers, finely chopped

1 jalapeno pepper, seeds and membrane removed, finely chopped

1 green onion, white and green parts, finely chopped

1 tsp (5 mL) fresh lemon juice

sea salt and freshly ground pepper to taste

Clam Chowder and Tea-Smoked Scallops

Serves 6

This recipe is inspired by traditional New England clam chowder but uses the best of B.C.'s seafood to make it our own. Pick up some fresh manila or little-neck clams along with pink swimming scallops for this creamy soup. In B.C., close to 2650 tons (2400 tonnes) of clams and 99 tons (90 tonnes) of scallops are produced each year, with 35% of the clam and 45% of the scallop harvest coming from shellfish aquaculture. The farming of shellfish is increasing every year and is expected to double by 2010, ensuring a sustainable supply of these delicacies.

Clams

2 cups (500 mL) white wine

2 cloves garlic, minced

sea salt and freshly ground pepper

4 lbs (2 kg) hard-shelled clams, well scrubbed

Scallops

2 Tbsp (30 mL) sugar

2 Tbsp (30 mL) rice

¼ cup (60 mL) oolong loose tea

6 scallops, shucked

olive oil for brushing scallops

In a large pot, bring wine and garlic to a boil, season lightly with salt and pepper, add clams and cook until they open, about 5 minutes. Discard any that do not open. Transfer remaining clams to a bowl. Reserve liquid (clam nectar), straining with a fine mesh colander.

Line a wide pot with foil (to save your pot and make clean up a snap). Sprinkle sugar, rice and tea on foil. Brush both sides of scallops lightly with oil. Place a wire rack, such as a small cooling rack, in pot and position scallops on rack so that they do not touch. Turn heat to high. When tea starts to smoke, cover pot tightly and reduce heat to low. Cook for 4 to 5 minutes. Turn off heat and let scallops rest an additional 2 to 3 minutes.

In a heavy pot, sauté onions in butter and oil until golden. Add vegetables, bay leaf and reserved clam nectar, and cover with stock. Simmer for 15 minutes, then add clams and cream. Simmer for 10 to 15 minutes more or until potatoes are cooked and soup is reduced and creamy. Ladle soup into individual bowls, and garnish each with a scallop and sprinkle of herbs.

Tip
For best results, time the scallops and chowder to be ready at the same time.

You can substitute ½ cup (125 mL) diced bacon, cooked until crispy, for the scallops. You could also dice the scallops and stir them into the soup, or use smaller bay scallops.

Chowder

2 medium onions, diced

¼ cup (60 mL) unsalted butter

1 Tbsp (15 mL) olive oil

2 cups (500 mL) diced celery

1 cup (250 mL) diced carrots

3 medium potatoes, peeled and diced

1 bay leaf

reserved clam nectar

fish or clam stock, enough to just cover vegetables

clams, as prepared opposite

2 cups (500 mL) heavy cream (32%)

scallops, as prepared opposite

¼ cup (60 mL) fresh herbs, such as parsley, thyme or tarragon

Dungeness Crab Cakes

Serves 6

It used to be a rite of passage for many youngsters to wade into the briny, sea-weed-rich waters of the Pacific during the summer months in search of Dungeness crab to bring home and boil for dinner. Nowadays, this crab is much easier to find at a local merchant such as T & T Market, the Lobster Man on Granville Island or even the infamous Crab Shop on Dollarton Highway. But one thing remains the same, the sweet-salty meat from a Dungeness crab is the best in the world and is almost perfect in its naked form. These crab cakes have just a few ingredients because we don't want to mask the flavour of this West Coast treasure!

1½ lbs (750 g) Dungeness crabmeat

1 yellow onion, diced

1 red bell pepper, diced

1 stalk celery, diced

2 Tbsp (30 mL) chopped fresh tarragon

zest from 1 lemon

pinch of cayenne pepper

1 Tbsp (15 mL) Worcestershire sauce

2 tsp (10 mL) Dijon mustard

sea salt and freshly ground pepper to taste

2 eggs, lightly beaten

seasoned fine bread-crumbs, enough to bind cakes, plus about 3 cups (750 mL) for dredging

flour, seasoned with sea salt and pepper

1 whole egg, beaten, for eggwash

Clean crabmeat, removing all cartilage and shells.

Sauté onion, bell pepper and celery until onion is translucent. Add tarragon, lemon zest, cayenne and Worcestershire sauce to vegetable mixture and let cool to room temperature.

Preheat oven to 375° F (190° C). Mix crabmeat, vegetable mixture, Dijon mustard, salt, pepper and 2 beaten eggs with enough breadcrumbs to hold cakes together. Form into ⅓ cup (75 mL) cakes. Dredge cakes in seasoned flour, then in eggwash and finally in seasoned breadcrumbs.

Pan-fry cakes until golden. Transfer to a baking sheet and finish cooking in oven, about 7 to 10 minutes. Serve hot with chipotle remoulade (see opposite).

Chipotle Remoulade

Chipotles are smoked jalapeño peppers, often found canned in adobe sauce. They are delicious and very spicy. Try the Mexican section at the supermarket, or find a Mexican specialty grocer.

Mix all ingredients together and refrigerate at least 4 hours or up to 1 week.

Tip

For best flavour, the chipotle remoulade must be made at least 4 hours before serving.

1½ cups (375 mL) mayonnaise (homemade is best, see p. 6)

1 Tbsp (15 mL) grainy mustard

chipotle peppers in adobe sauce, minced, about 1 tsp (5 mL) or to taste

½ cup (125 mL) finely diced green onions

1 Tbsp (15 mL) chopped capers

1 tsp (5 mL) minced garlic

¼ cup (60 mL) finely chopped parsley

juice of ¼ lemon

sea salt and freshly cracked pepper to taste

Panko and Coconut Spot Prawns

Serves 6

Spot prawns are named for the distinctive white spots that adorn their shells. Highly regarded for their size and firm, sweet flesh, spot prawns are the largest of the seven shrimp species caught commercially in B.C.'s coastal waters; females are known to grow to 9 inches (23 centimetres) in length or more. Spot prawns are usually sold fresh for just over 11 weeks beginning in May, mostly in B.C., but they are available frozen year-round. Over 90% of the catch is exported to Japan, although domestic consumption is increasing as more Canadian chefs discover the spot prawns' great taste.

1 cup (250 mL) flour

sea salt and freshly ground pepper

3 eggs, beaten

1 cup (250 mL) panko (Japanese bread crumbs)

½ cup (125 mL) shredded unsweetened coconut

24 spot prawns, shelled, deveined, tail on

4 cups (1 L) peanut oil, for frying

½ cup (125 mL) Thai chili dipping sauce

Place flour in a bowl or shallow baking dish, and season with salt and pepper. Beat eggs in a separate bowl. Combine panko and coconut in another shallow dish. Dredge prawns first in flour, then in beaten eggs and finally coat in panko mixture. Carefully lay prawns out in a single layer on a baking sheet.

Pour oil into a heavy-bottomed skillet and heat to 360° F (180° C); if you do not have a thermometer, test oil with a cube of bread—it should turn golden in under 2 minutes. Cook prawns in small batches until golden, about 2 minutes, then transfer to a plate lined with a paper towel. Serve hot with dipping sauce.

Tip
Whenever possible, buy your prawns with heads on. Keeping them whole is worth the extra work and ensures the flavourful juices are retained in the flesh. Thaw frozen prawns in the refrigerator overnight and use immediately.

Panko is a Japanese-style breadcrumb that is now popular enough to be widely available in most grocery stores (or visit an Asian specialty grocer). It is an ultra-white, extra-coarse breadcrumb that stays particularly crispy when fried.

Wild B.C. Sablefish and Lentils with Vinaigrette

Serves 4

Sablefish is one of the hottest items on many of B.C.'s top restaurant menus. Sablefish, also known as black cod or butterfish, is caught in the deep waters far off the coast of B.C. Traditionally, most sablefish has been exported to Japan and Hong Kong, but it is now commonly available at many fishmongers around the province. Whether you buy it smoked or fresh, its sweet flavour and large white flakes are always sure to please. This recipe uses fresh herbs to complement the rich, oily texture of fresh sablefish.

4 x 4 oz (125 g) sablefish

splash of olive oil

1 cup (250 mL) cooked red lentils (see Tip)

¼ cup (60 mL) olive oil

¼ cup (60 mL) lemon juice

1 Tbsp (15 mL) fresh thyme, chopped

1 Tbsp (15 mL) fresh chives, chopped

1 Tbsp (15 mL) orange zest

sea salt and freshly ground pepper

½ lb (250 g) mixed salad greens with fresh herbs

Season sablefish with salt and pepper. Heat a small pan over medium-high heat and add a splash of oil. Sear fish, about 2 to 3 minutes per side. Remove from heat and set aside.

Mix warmed, cooked lentils in a bowl with olive oil, lemon juice, thyme, chives, orange zest, salt and pepper together.

Serve grilled sablefish on a bed of lentils and mixed salad with fresh herbs.

Tip

To cook lentils, pour 1 cup (250 mL) of cleaned, dry lentils into 3 cups (750 mL) salted, boiling water. Reduce heat and simmer until the lentils until al dente, about 20 minutes. One cup (250 mL) of dry lentils makes 2 to 2½ cups (500 to 625 mL) of cooked lentils.

Pacific Scallops with Back Bacon and Vanilla

Serves 4

Pacific scallops are always a treat (when you can get them), but when paired with back bacon and a hint of vanilla, they are incredible. For this recipe, try to get your hands on some back bacon from the "House of Bacon" at Oyama Sausage. With more than 90% of its products made using locally raised B.C. pork, Oyama makes some of the finest tasting bacon you will find. And with more than a dozen varieties, if back bacon is not your preference, you can choose from many other kinds. Oyama prides itself on producing the highest quality products and even goes so far as to ensure that its pigs are raised using only the finest feed, including organic hazelnuts, to ensure the best possible flavour in the meat!

⅔ cup (150 mL) diced back bacon

2 Tbsp (30 mL) minced shallots

1 cup (250 mL) dry B.C. sparkling wine

½ vanilla bean pod

½ tsp (2 mL) champagne vinegar, plus extra for dressing

1 cup (250 mL) cold unsalted butter, cut into small pieces

sea salt and freshly ground white pepper to taste

12 Pacific scallops

1 bunch watercress, tough stems removed, cleaned and spun dry

1 Tbsp (15 mL) olive oil, plus extra for dressing

fresh chives for garnish

In a medium saucepan, sauté back bacon until crispy. Set bacon aside and stir in shallots, sparkling wine, vanilla bean pod and seeds, and bring to a boil. Reduce heat to medium-low and simmer until you have about ¼ cup (60 mL) of liquid remaining. Stir in champagne vinegar and remove vanilla pod. Turn heat down to very low and, little by little, whisk in butter, 1 piece at a time. Continue until all butter pieces have been added and sauce will coat back of a spoon. Stir in bacon, and season sauce with salt and pepper. Keep sauce warm but off direct heat until ready to serve.

Season scallops on all sides with salt and pepper. Place olive oil in a large pan over medium-high heat. When oil is hot, add scallops and sear for 2 to 3 minutes, until nicely caramelized. Turn scallops over and cook for an additional 3 minutes.

For dressing, toss watercress in a bowl with a splash of olive oil and champagne vinegar, and season with salt and pepper. Serve scallops immediately with sauce, watercress and chives.

Tip

To get the most flavour out of a vanilla bean pod, carefully slice it open and scrape out the tiny seeds; use both seeds and pod in the recipe.

What we call "back bacon" is known south of the border and overseas as "Canadian bacon." Praised for its leanness, high quality and smoky flavour, it is the choice bacon for fine hotels and restaurants. Peameal bacon is another extra-lean, very popular Canadian bacon, often roasted whole and served with a maple glaze or sliced and served instead of ham on eggs Benedict.

Grilled Beef Tenderloin with Sautéed Chanterelles

Serves 4

Most British Columbians associate quality Canadian beef with our neighbours to the east, where Alberta has reigned supreme in the cattle industry for decades. However, the Blue Goose Cattle Company in the southern Cariboo is trying to change that. On over 250,000 acres (101,000 hectares) of land, Blue Goose raises both premium and organic beef that is finding its way onto restaurant menus and into high-end butcher shops around the province. What sets this high-quality, pasture-raised beef apart from others is the taste, and carnivores will find that Blue Goose is worth the premium price.

4 beef tenderloin medallions, about 6 to 8 oz (170 to 250 g) each

olive oil, for brushing

2 tsp (10 mL) kosher salt

freshly ground black pepper

Mushrooms

1 to 2 Tbsp (15 to 30 mL) olive oil

3 shallots, sliced

1 lb (500 g) fresh chanterelles

1 clove garlic, minced

½ cup (125 mL) white wine

1 cup (250 mL) parsley, chopped

¼ cup (60 mL) chives, chopped

sea salt and freshly ground black pepper

Remove beef medallions from refrigerator 15 minutes before cooking.

To prepare the mushrooms, heat olive oil in a skillet over medium-high heat and sauté the shallots until soft. Add chanterelles, garlic and continue to sauté for 5 to 7 minutes, then add white wine and cook until the liquid evaporates. Remove from heat and stir in parsley and chives. Season with salt and pepper. Set aside.

Prepare a grill or a stove-top grill pan with a medium-high heat fire. Brush beef lightly with olive oil and season with salt and pepper and place on the grill and cook, without moving it, until nice grill marks appear, about 4 minutes. Turn the medallions and continue to grill until an instant-read thermometer inserted into the medallions sideways registers about 120° F (50° C), about 3 to 4 minutes more. Set aside on a cutting board to rest for 5 minutes before serving.

Divide medallions among plates and spoon on the mushrooms.

Mu Shu Duck with Peaches and Daikon

Serves 4

Game birds such as geese, wild turkey, prairie chicken, partridge and grouse were an important food source for Canada's indigenous peoples, and early B.C. settlers soon learned to hunt them as well. Game birds have always been abundant here, at least seasonally. One of the province's leading organic duck producers is Polderside Farm in the Fraser Valley. This farm offers specialties such as organic, free-range duck, chicken and eggs. Their duck is available at the farm gate, as well as on the menus of B.C.'s finer restaurants. The duck in this recipe is combined with ripe, juicy peaches and daikon (Japanese radish), showcasing the multicultural aspect of B.C.'s cuisine.

Duck

8 oz (250 g) duck breast, about 2 breasts, cut into strips

3 Tbsp (45 mL) rice vinegar

2 Tbsp (30 mL) soy sauce

1 tsp (5 mL) sesame oil

1 Tbsp (15 mL) garlic, minced

1 Tbsp (15 mL) fresh ginger, finely chopped

grape seed or canola oil for stir frying

½ cup (125 mL) green onions, finely sliced

Daikon

1 daikon radish, 4-inch (10 cm) piece, grated

1 Tbsp (15 mL) rice vinegar

½ tsp (2 mL) sugar

1 Tbsp (15 mL) green onion, finely sliced

In a bowl, toss the duck with the rice vinegar, soy sauce, sesame oil, garlic and ginger. Cover and marinate, refrigerated, for 2 hours. In another bowl, toss the daikon with rice vinegar, sugar and green onion. Set aside.

Heat a splash of grape seed oil in a wok (or heavy-bottomed pan) and add the marinated duck strips. Stir fry over high heat until

browned and cooked through, about 3 minutes. Remove from the pan, toss with green onions and set aside. Reduce the heat to medium and cook peaches in the wok for 5 minutes, and set aside. Add a splash of oil to the wok and cook eggs, sunny side up.

Serve duck, daikon, peaches, eggs and enoki mushrooms on a platter along with side serving plates. Spread a spoonful of hoisin sauce on a flatbread and place some meat, peaches and vegetables on top, roll up and enjoy.

2 fresh peaches, cut into eighths

4 large eggs

4 oz (125 g) fresh enoki mushrooms

hoisin sauce

1 package store-bought flatbread, such as chapati

Pemberton Potato Salad

Serves 4 to 6

The Pemberton Valley, north of Whistler, is home to rich agricultural lands that have become world famous for their seed potatoes as well as other root crops. In the late 1960s, the Pemberton Valley actually became the first farming community in the world to successfully grow virus-free seed potatoes. Today, many of the local farms, such as North Arm Farm owned by ski-patroller-turned-farmer-turned-mayor Jordon Sturdy, grow crops including corn, berries, flowers, squash and more. For this recipe, try to use Pemberton fingerling potatoes for their rich and buttery texture.

2 lbs (1 kg) potatoes, scrubbed

sea salt

2 carrots, diced

2 celery stalks, diced

1 x 8 oz (250 g) jar arti-choke hearts, well drained and rinsed, then drained again and cut into eighths

1 green onion, white part only, finely chopped

1 red pepper, diced into small pieces

6 black olives, pitted and cut into slivers

6 baby gherkins, thinly sliced

¼ cup (60 mL) parsley, finely chopped

1 Tbsp (15 ml) capers, drained and chopped

¼ tsp (1 mL) sea salt

freshly ground black pepper

mayonnaise (see Essential Ingredients, p. 6)

Cook the potatoes in gently boiling salted water, until just tender. Once cooled, peel the potatoes, cut into smallish cubes and set aside in a bowl. Meanwhile, cook the carrots in gently boiling salted water for 5 minutes, then drain and refresh with cold water and dry them on a paper towel. Combine carrots and the rest of the ingredients with the potatoes and mix enough mayonnaise for a nice creamy texture. Taste and adjust seasonings. Serve or chill until ready to serve.

Summer Squash Ratatouille

Serves 4 as a main course, 6 as a side dish

This summer dish is a traditional French Provençal stew, and by adding herbs de Provence you will achieve an authentic flavour with hints of lavender from the French hillsides. The difference between summer squash and winter squash is in their shelf life. Winter squash, such as pumpkins, develop hard rinds and can be stored for months, whereas summer squash, such as zucchini, are best eaten before they mature and develop a bitter flavour. In B.C., summer squash is plentiful with many home gardeners growing more than they can ever use, so the next time your neighbour gives you zucchini, try using it for this recipe.

1 medium eggplant, 2½ lbs (1.2 kg),
cut into ½ in (1 cm) cubes

olive oil for cooking

1 lb (500 g) assorted summer squash,
as much variety as possible,
cut into ½ in (1 cm) slices

2 medium onions, sliced

2 red bell peppers, seeded and
cut into ½ in (1 cm) strips

3 ripe but firm tomatoes about 1 lb (500 g),
seeded and quartered

2 cloves garlic, minced

⅓ cup (75 mL) of a mixture of chopped fresh
rosemary, thyme, basil, fennel and marjoram

pinch of dried lavender

sea salt and freshly ground
black pepper to taste

French bread

Lay the eggplant cubes on paper towels and sprinkle with salt. Let them sit for 15 minutes, then rinse and pat dry.

Have a large bowl ready. Heat a splash of olive oil in a large skillet or casserole over medium heat. Add the eggplant chunks and cook until they start to soften, remove from pan and set aside in the bowl to make room for the next vegetable. Add more olive oil, as needed, and continue with the squash, onions and peppers separately.

Return all vegetables to pan; add tomatoes, garlic and herbs. Season with salt and

pepper and stir to mix. Simmer over medium heat until much of the liquid is evaporated, about 10 minutes, then cover, turn heat to medium low and cook until the vegetables are tender, about 45 minutes to 1 hour, stirring occasionally to prevent sticking. Serve at room temperature with crusty French bread.

Tip
Squash blossoms are also edible and make a great vessel for stuffing and deep frying. Make sure you choose the male stems (but leave a few for pollination) and leave the fruit-bearing females for an abundant summer supply.

Char-grilled Corn with Jalapeño Lime Butter

Many of B.C.'s warmest regions, including the Okanagan Valley and eastern Fraser Valley, produce the province's sweetest corn because of the combination of hot summer days and cooler nights—optimal conditions for increasing the sugar content. In B.C., we produce more than 40 million pounds (18 million kilograms) of corn each year, but only a quarter of it goes unprocessed. Sadly, in our quest for sweet corn, we have lost many of the hundreds of varieties that were once common. This recipe combines one of summer's greatest treasures with a Mexican inspired butter that will have you heating up the barbecue all summer long!

ears of corn

jalapeño lime butter (see below)

lime wedges

sea salt to taste

Jalapeño Lime Butter

1 cup (250 mL) unsalted butter, softened

1 jalapeño pepper, seeded and finely chopped

zest from 1 lime

1 clove garlic, minced

1 tsp (5 mL) sea salt

Preheat the barbecue to medium-high heat. Peel back the husks, leaving them attached, and remove the silk from the corn. Rewrap, tying with butcher twine or kitchen string if necessary. Barbecue for about 10 minutes, turning to cook all sides. If husks start to burn, spritz with water.

Serve hot corn with rounds of the jalapeño lime butter, lime wedges and sea salt.

Jalapeño Lime Butter
Mix the ingredients together in a bowl or in a food processor. Wrap in plastic and shape into a cylinder about an inch (2.5 cm) in diameter, and refrigerate.

Sweet corn, which is the corn that we eat fresh, is the result of a gene mutation in field corn. This mutation occurred in the 1800s in the United States and prevented sugar in the kernel from being converted to starch.

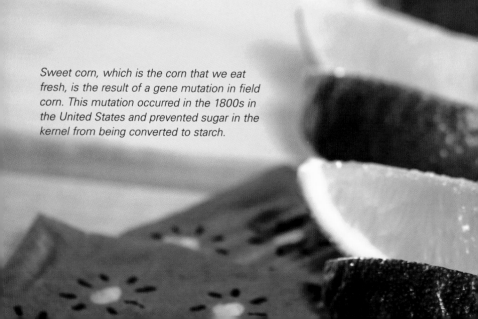

Tip
To keep the sugars from turning to starch, keep freshly picked corn as cool as possible and enjoy it soon after harvesting. Fresh corn can be steamed, boiled or grilled, and older corn can be cut from the cob and added to soups and stews.

Barbecued B.C. Peaches with Camembert

Serves 6

Juicy and sweet, British Columbian peaches are at their best in mid-July. A road trip through B.C.'s southern Okanagan region, Canada's most important peach-growing area, is incomplete without a stop at one of the many fruit stands that line the roads of the Similkameen Valley. Just one bite into the yellow or white flesh is truly a taste of summer in B.C. To experience the best of B.C.'s peaches, be sure to head out to the Penticton Peach Festival, held every year in mid-August. The festival originated in 1947 and is now a five-day extravaganza filled with parades, live music and much more.

6 peaches, pitted and sliced in half

2 Tbsp (30 mL) canola or grape seed oil

1 Tbsp (15 mL) honey

pinch of sea salt

pinch of pepper

4 oz (125 g) Camembert, cut into wedges

6 fresh basil leaves

Preheat barbecue to medium-high. Combine oil, honey, salt and pepper in a bowl. Brush peaches with glaze and grill flesh side down for 3 minutes. Place peaches flesh side up on a baking sheet and place a basil leaf and a wedge of Camembert on top of each peach. Return the peaches on baking sheet to the barbecue, close the lid and cook until the cheese is melted, about 5 minutes.

Peaches are the stone fruit from a tree that originated in China, where peaches are an important symbol for a long life and immortality.

Iced Tea with Fresh Mint

Serves 4

There are two traditional types of iced tea—sweetened and unsweetened. In B.C., the general preference seems to be for the sweetened variety, with many variations possible because of our province's obsession with all things healthy and ethnic. Beyond the traditional black tea, you can make iced tea using roiboos tea from South Africa, green teas from China, chai from India or even matcha from Japan. The Tea Shop at Granville Island offers one of B.C.'s best selections of fine quality teas along with the best prices. Don't forget to add mint or even a couple of slices of orange or lemon to improve the flavour even more.

6 cups (1.5 L) cold water

5 level tsp (25 mL) good quality, loose tea

⅔ cup (150 mL) white sugar, or to taste

handful of fresh mint, rinsed and patted dry

1 orange or lemon

Bring water to a boil. Place the tea in a pitcher and pour the boiling water over the tea. Let infuse for 30 minutes.

Stir in sugar to dissolve and strain tea into a clean pitcher. Add the remaining water.

Bruise the mint by crushing it lightly with a rolling pin or the bottom of a glass and place in the pitcher.

Chill tea for at least 1 hour. Remove mint and serve with a wedge of lime or lemon and a sprig of mint, if desired.

Some people call the alcohol-spiked version of iced tea "iced tea on a stick." Iced coffee is also a popular summer drink available homemade or purchased from fine coffee shops throughout the province.

Birchwood Dairy Yogurt and Honey Semifreddo

Serves 4 to 6

This recipe draws inspiration from the numerous ice cream and gelato shops that service just about every neighbourhood in Vancouver. Making semifreddo is easier than making ice cream and is as delicious as the homemade gelato available around the corner. But where to get B.C. yogurt? Birchwood Dairy is a family-owned farm in the Fraser Valley that produces some fine dairy products, including yogurt. The perfect combination of slightly tart and super creamy, this is the yogurt of choice to blend with any premium B.C. honey, and it will keep your guests coming back for more!

2¼ cups (560 mL) heavy cream (32%)

5 egg yolks

½ cup (125 mL) honey

½ cup (125 mL) unflavoured yogurt

In a mixer, whisk cream to stiff peaks. Transfer the whipped cream into another bowl and set aside. Clean and dry the mixing bowl and whisk yolks with honey until pale yellow and thickened. Fold in yogurt. Then fold in whipped cream.

Line a mould with plastic wrap. Place filling into the mould. Cover and freeze for 24 hours. Remove semifreddo from the freezer just before serving. Top with your favourite berries.

Semifreddo is Italian for "half-cold" and describes the half-frozen or chilled nature of this delicious confection.

roodies in B.C. are enamoured with chutneys and jams that pair well with cheese plates, roasted meats and more, and this is a perfect recipe for all these applications. The caramelized flavour of this jam comes from a long cooking process, which brings out the sugars in the onion and causes them to caramelize. For this recipe, we have paired it with a cheese tray as part of an after-dinner treat, but it works equally well as an appetizer or even spooned on top of grilled scallops.

¼ cup (60 mL) olive oil

6 medium sweet onions, sliced thinly

pinch sea salt

1 Tbsp (15 mL) balsamic vinegar

¼ cup (60 mL) port

sprig of fresh thyme

½ cup (120 mL) muscovado sugar

1 tsp (5 mL) mustard seeds

½ tsp (2 mL) red pepper flakes

¼ cup (60 mL) tomato, finely chopped

Melt the oil in heavy frying pan. Add the onions and sauté until slightly brown. Season with salt. Reduce the heat, then continue to cook, stirring constantly, until caramelized and tender. Add the remaining ingredients, except the tomato, and cook on low heat for 30 minutes, stirring occasionally. Add the tomato and cook for 15 more minutes. Let cool and store in a jar in the refrigerator. Keeps for 2 weeks refrigerated.

Try onion jam on pizzas and sandwiches.

Cherry Pie
Serves 6 to 8

Nothing is more B.C. than cherry pie in the summer. The province's farmers produce more than 12 million pounds (5.5 million kilograms) of sweet cherries and 2.2 million pounds (1 million kilograms) of sour cherries each year, with varieties such as Bing, Lambert, Van, Lapins and Sweethearts. With the proliferation of B.C.'s wine industry, many cherries are being turned into fabulous fruit wines such as Elephant Island's Stella Cherry Port and Forbidden Fruit's Cerise D'Eve. If you can find these treasures, they will add a great splash of flavour to this pie or serve as the perfect accompaniment to some great dark chocolate.

6 cups (1.5 L) fresh pitted cherries

¾ cup (175 mL) sugar

juice from a lemon

2 Tbsp (30 mL) cornstarch

pastry (see opposite)

Preheat oven to 400° F (200° C). In a medium saucepan, mix cherries and sugar and cook over medium-low heat until most of the juice from the cherries has reduced, about 15 minutes. Stir the lemon juice and cornstarch together in a small bowl and add to the cherries. Cook, stirring until thick, about 7 minutes. Remove from heat and let cool to room temperature.

Pour cherry filling into a prepared pastry crust and bake for 10 minutes. Reduce heat to 375° F (190° C) and bake for 20 to 30 minutes or until pastry is golden brown. Let it cool before serving.

Great Pie Crust

Mix flour, salt and sugar in a bowl. Using your cheese grater, grate frozen butter into flour mixture. Toss lightly to distribute butter and add lemon juice and enough water for dough just to come together. Divide in half, wrap each piece in plastic wrap and flatten into a disc. Chill for at least 30 minutes before using. Makes enough for a double-crusted pie.

2½ cups (625 mL) flour

1 tsp (5 mL) sea salt

1 Tbsp (15 mL) sugar

1 cup (250 mL) unsalted butter, frozen

1 Tbsp (15 mL) lemon juice

about ⅓ cup (75 mL) ice water

Tip

To make a lattice top, roll out and cut the remaining piece of dough into 1-inch (2.5 cm) strips. Interlock the strips in a criss-cross weave over the pie filling and press the strips onto the edges of the bottom crust. Brush the pastry lightly with a glaze made with 1 beaten egg and 2 Tbsp (30 mL) milk.

Raspberry Tart

Serves 6 to 8

Fragrantly sweet and subtly tart, raspberries are a favourite B.C. fruit. A member of the rose family, raspberries grow in almost all parts of the province, but more than 98% are produced in the Abbotsford area of the Fraser Valley. A fantastic crop of wild raspberries grows in central B.C. each year. An enterprising young man named Ryan Veitch has formed a company called Wild Berry Wholesome Foods, whose delectable line of jams and jellies feature only hand-picked wild fruits from around the province.

Crust

1¼ cups (310 mL)
all-purpose flour

¼ cup (60 mL) sugar

½ cup (125 mL) or 1 stick
unsalted butter, cold and
cut into pieces

2 to 3 Tbsp (30 to 45 mL)
cold water

Filling

2 x 8 oz containers (275 g)
mascarpone,
room temperature

½ cup (125 mL) sugar

1 tsp (5 mL) vanilla

3 cups (750 mL) raspberries,
picked over

Glaze

1 x 8 oz (250 mL) jar of
apple jelly

For the crust, place flour, sugar and butter in a food processor and blend until mixture resembles coarse meal. Add 2 Tbsp (30 mL) of the water until incorporated. Add enough remaining water, if necessary, until mixture comes together but is still crumbly. Wrap dough in plastic and refrigerate for 1 hour.

Preheat oven to 350° F (175° C). Press crust mixture evenly onto bottom and sides of an 11-inch (28 cm) tart pan with removable fluted rim or 6 to 8 individual tart tins. Prick crust with a fork, line it with parchment and weigh it down with pie weights or dried beans. Bake in middle of oven until golden, about 15 minutes. Let cool to room temperature and chill for 1 hour in refrigerator.

Make the filling while the crust chills. In a bowl, using an electric mixer, beat mascarpone, sugar and vanilla together until smooth. Pour filling into chilled crust, spreading evenly, and arrange raspberries on top.

If keeping the tart longer than a day, brush raspberries lightly with a glaze of warmed apple jelly.

Tip
When out picking raspberries in your yard or favourite U-pick farm, be sure to keep them as cool as possible (ideally, pick them during cooler times of the day or on a cloudy day), and store them unwashed.

Raspberries are healthy, antioxidant-rich berries high in ellagic acid—the same family of tannins that make wine, green tea and fruit such as pomegranates an important part of a healthy lifestyle.

Fruit Smoothie

Serves 1

A fruit smoothie is a great and healthy breakfast for people on the go. Smoothies are the perfect excuse (although who needs one?) to use some of B.C.'s yummiest treats—from fruit such as blueberries, strawberries or peaches, to yogurt from Island Farms or Birchwood Dairy, to honey from Chilliwack Valley Honey. Some of our favourites include peach, pineapple and coconut and blueberry banana. Smoothies can also be made using frozen yogurt, frozen bananas, ice cream or even soy milk. Try a shot of Baileys Irish Cream in a chocolate banana smoothie for a weekend indulgence.

1 banana, peeled, cut and frozen

¾ cup (175 mL) fresh or frozen berries

¼ cup (60 mL) coconut milk

1 cup (250 mL) vanilla soy milk

1 Tbsp (15 mL) almond butter

¼ cup (60 mL) crushed ice

Purée all ingredients in a blender until smooth.

Tip
Coconut milk from a can will keep in the fridge for 4 to 5 days.

Fruit smoothies are perfect for breakfast. Add some flax seed or bran for a really healthy kick.

Lentil and Roasted Similkameen Valley Garlic Soup

Serves 4 to 6

Lentils are in the group of plants known as pulses or legumes, where the seed is grown in a pod; other examples are chickpeas and beans. Lentils are one of our favourite legumes because of their short cooking time and high protein and fibre concentrations. Surprisingly, Canada is the world's largest exporter of lentils, with the majority of lentils exported to India. While B.C. is not one of the top producing provinces for this export, we do have farmers in the Fraser Valley who produce unique varieties.

½ tsp (2 mL) cinnamon

¼ tsp (1 mL) cloves

1 Tbsp (15 mL) cumin

2 tsp (10 mL) olive oil

1 cup (250 mL) onions, chopped

½ cup (125 mL) carrot, diced

1 large bay leaf

½ inch (1 cm) piece fresh ginger, peeled and chopped

2 cups (500 mL) dried red lentils, rinsed

water

1 bulb roasted garlic (see p. 127), cloves squeezed out

1 Tbsp (15 mL) apple cider vinegar

2 tsp (10 mL) cilantro, chopped

salt and freshly ground pepper to taste

finely sliced chives for garnish

In a small pan, toast the cinnamon, cloves and cumin until very fragrant, about 1 to 2 minutes. Set aside.

In a medium-sized pot, heat oil over medium-high heat and sauté onions until translucent. Add carrots, bay leaf, ginger with the toasted cinnamon, cloves and cumin and sauté about 2 minutes. Add lentils and add enough water to cover by 1 inch (2.5 cm) and cook 30 to 45 minutes, or until the lentils are completely soft. Purée lentils and roasted garlic in a blender. Stir in the apple cider vinegar and cilantro. Season with salt and plenty of pepper. Garnish each serving with chives.

Spiced Parsnip and Cauliflower Soup

Serves 4 to 6

With its elegant ivory colour and sweet, complex flavour, the parsnip is the queen of root vegetables. It can be used in everything from soups to main courses, and when combined with some melted butter and brown sugar, honey or birch syrup for a side dish, it tastes just like candy. The parsnip came to North America from Europe in the 17th century; however, it has never gained great popularity here in B.C. This situation is unfortunate, given that this root crop is especially well suited to a short growing season in a cool climate in areas of B.C. like Pemberton and the Fraser Valley. The parsnip is best eaten late in autumn, once it has benefited from exposure to frost.

2 to 3 Tbsp (15 to 30 mL) olive oil

1 Tbsp (15 mL) yellow mustard seeds

2 onions, finely chopped

2 garlic cloves, minced

1 tsp (5 mL) fresh ginger, finely chopped

1 Tbsp (15 mL) turmeric

1 tsp (5 mL) cardamom

1 tsp (5 mL) cumin

1 lb (500 g) cauliflower, trimmed and cut into florets

1 lb (500 g) parsnips, peeled and cut into chunks roughly the same size as the cauliflower

2 cups (500 mL) vegetable or chicken stock or water

1⅔ cups (400 mL) coconut milk

sea salt and freshly ground pepper to taste

1 Tbsp (15 mL) fresh cilantro, finely chopped

Heat the oil in a large saucepan over medium-high heat. When the oil is hot, add the mustard seeds and cook until they begin to pop. Add onion, garlic and ginger, and cook for a couple of minutes until the onion is soft and translucent. Add turmeric, cardamom and cumin. Add cauliflower and parsnip and cook the mixture while stirring for a couple of minutes. Add the stock or water to the pan and bring it slowly to a boil. Skim off any scum that comes to the top and reduce the soup to a simmer. Leave it to cook gently for 30 minutes, stirring regularly.

The soup is ready when the cauliflower is cooked and tender. Stir in the coconut milk. Purée the soup in the blender until smooth and return it to a clean saucepan. Season the soup with salt and pepper, garnish with cilantro and serve.

Tip
Parsnips are best stored in a very cold location or in the refrigerator.

For a different snack, try making parsnip chips! Peel 3 or 4 parsnips lengthwise with a sharp vegetable peeler into long paper thin strips, until you've reached the central core. Heat oil in a medium-sized saucepan to 350˚ F (175˚ C) and drop parsnip strips in small batches and fry for 1 minute until crisp and golden. Drain on paper towels, season with sea salt and serve.

Pumpkin Fondue

Serves 12 as an appetizer

Just about everyone who got married during the 1970s received at least one fondue pot for a wedding present. Three decades later, fondues have come back as a tasty, special part of a social gathering. They can be savoury or sweet, and there are many variations of the traditional cheese fondue. For example, an oil or broth can be used for meat fondues, and chocolate fondue is another popular version usually using fruit or cake for dipping. The following pumpkin fondue is a departure from the traditional, but it will have your guests talking!

1 sugar pumpkin, about 3 to 4 lbs (1.5 to 2 kg)

2 Tbsp (30 mL) unsalted butter

1 small onion, finely chopped

1 clove garlic, minced

1 cup (250 mL) dry white wine

pinch of freshly grated nutmeg

2 Tbsp (30 mL) flour

¼ cup (60 mL) fresh sage, chopped

2 cups (500 mL) grated aged white cheddar cheese

½ cup (125 mL) sour cream

sea salt and freshly ground pepper to taste

Preheat oven to 350° F (175° C). Pierce the top of the pumpkin with a knife 3 or 4 times, and bake for 20 minutes. Let cool for 10 minutes. Remove top a quarter of the way down, forming a lid. Scoop out the seeds and fibres and set aside. Increase oven temperature to 375° F (190° C).

Melt butter in a medium saucepan and sauté onion for 5 minutes. Add garlic and cook until softened. Add white wine and bring to a simmer. Finally, add nutmeg, flour, sage and cheddar cheese and stir until the cheese is melted. Pour into the pumpkin, cover with its lid and bake for 20 minutes, until the mixture is hot. Remove from oven and stir in sour cream. Adjust salt and pepper, if needed, and serve with skewers of crusty bread for dipping and spoons for scooping out the delicious pumpkin flesh.

Coq au Vin with Okanagan Pinot Noir

Serves 6

British Columbia wines are earning an excellent reputation for quality within Canada and abroad. The Okanagan Valley lies at the same latitude as northern French and German vineyards. The Northern Okanagan is producing some world-class, Alsatian-style whites, while the sandy desert soils of the south are ideal for varietals such as Pinot Gris, Chardonnay, Merlot, Cabernet Sauvignon and Pinot Noir. While many people think of Coq au Vin as a dish using red wine, it is actually meant to be a dish using the "local" wine, so many regions of France have variations of the dish—even Coq au Champagne! In this version we have chosen to use Thomas Reid Chicken from the Fraser Valley and an Okanagan Pinot Noir, but the choice is up to you!

2 Tbsp (30 mL) unsalted butter

⅔ cup (150 mL) bacon, diced

1 free-range chicken, 3 to 4 lbs (1.5 to 2 kg), cut into 8 pieces

2 medium onions, chopped

1 carrot, chopped

1 cup celery root, diced

2 garlic cloves, sliced

2 Tbsp (30 mL) flour

1 bottle Okanagan Pinot Noir (750 mL)

4 sprigs of fresh thyme

8 cups (2 L) chicken stock

3 bay leaves

¼ cup (60 mL) unsalted butter

2 cups (500 mL) small white button mushrooms, left whole

sea salt and freshly ground pepper

Melt the butter in heavy-bottomed casserole and add the bacon. Cook over medium heat until bacon is crisp, drain on paper towels and place into a large bowl.

Season the chicken pieces with salt and pepper and cook them in the bacon drippings until they are golden brown. Transfer to the bowl with the bacon. Add the onions, carrot and celery root to the pan and cook slowly on medium heat, stirring from time to time, until the onion is translucent. Add the garlic, then stir in the flour and let cook for 3 to 5 minutes. Add the chicken, bacon, red wine, thyme and enough chicken stock to cover the chicken. Bring to a boil, reduce heat and cook, partially covered, for 45 minutes to 1 hour or until the chicken is tender.

Meanwhile, melt the remaining butter in a small pan and sauté the mushrooms until golden. Season them lightly with salt and pepper, then add to the chicken. To serve, ladle some of the sauce into a saucepan and reduce over high heat until thick and glossy.

Serve the chicken and sauce over hot buttered noodles.

This classic French dish, originally traced back to ancient Gaul and the times of Julius Caesar, is hearty and rich, with local chicken and fragrant herbs stewed in red wine. Age is definitely a virtue—in this recipe, using an older bird produces a richer flavour.

Apple-roasted Pheasant

Serves 4

Apples and pheasant paired together make the perfect fall dish to celebrate a successful growing season. The flavours of the apple and herbs will penetrate the meat of the pheasant and lend an almost sweet taste to the bird. For extra flavour, you could also roast the pheasant on your barbecue and use some apple wood chips under the grate to add some smoky apple notes to the dish. This recipe can also be made with other poultry such as quail or chicken, and you could even experiment with other local fruits such as quince or pears.

4 pheasant breasts, skin on, wing attached

sea salt and freshly cracked black pepper

1 Tbsp (15 mL) butter

1 Tbsp (15 mL) grape seed oil or olive oil

4 cups (32 oz) Pink Lady apples, peeled and sliced

¼ cup (60 mL) honey

1 Tbsp (15 mL) garlic, minced

1 tsp (5 mL) cinnamon

1 tsp (5 mL) cloves

juice of half a lemon

Preheat oven to 425° F (220° C). Season pheasant with salt and pepper. Heat butter and oil in an ovenproof sauté pan that is large enough to comfortably fit all the meat. On medium-high heat, sear pheasant breasts, skin side down, for 3 to 4 minutes until golden brown. Set aside.

Combine all the remaining ingredients in a mixing bowl and sauté in the same pan as the pheasant. When the apples are nicely caramelized, about 5 minutes, place the pheasant on top, skin sides up, and roast in the oven for 10 to 12 minutes, until the meat is cooked through.

Serve the breasts atop a spoonful of the caramelized apples.

Native to Japan and China, the pheasant is a member of the Phasianidae family of birds, which includes the quail and the peacock. Terrestrial birds that can be distinguished by the male's ornate plumage, pheasants were introduced into North America in 1881.

Sweet and Sour Pork

Serves 6

Chinese immigrants began to settle in British Columbia in large numbers beginning with the Fraser River Gold Rush of 1858. In the early to mid-1880s, 17,000 Chinese men came to Canada to build the western section of the Canadian Pacific Railway. After the last spike was driven, these hard-working immigrants were left unemployed and received no assistance from the Canadian government. Using their strong cultural ties to food, many of these men opened restaurants, often along the route of the CPR. Today, Vancouver is home to one of North America's largest Chinatowns and approximately 18% of the current population in the Greater Vancouver area are of Chinese ethnicity. Many of the region's Chinese restaurants are now reputed to be some of the best in the world!

2 Tbsp (30 mL) cornstarch

1 lb (500 g) boneless pork loin rib, cut into bite-sized pieces

2 egg yolks

1 Tbsp (15 mL) soy sauce

2 tsp (10 mL) sea salt

⅔ cup (150 mL) rice wine vinegar

¼ cup (60 mL) white wine

⅓ cup (75 mL) sugar

3 cloves garlic, minced

2 Tbsp (30 mL) grated fresh ginger

½ small pineapple, peeled, cored, quartered and sliced

1 small tomato, diced

½ cup (125 mL) julienned red pepper

1 tsp (5 mL) cinnamon

vegetable oil for frying

¼ cup (60 mL) each cornstarch and flour, sifted together into a bowl

1 cup (250 mL) snow peas

In a bowl, add cornstarch to 1 Tbsp (15 mL) cold water and mix well. Add pork, egg yolks, soy sauce and 1 tsp (5 mL) salt. Toss well, and refrigerate overnight.

Place vinegar, wine, sugar and remaining salt into a pan and bring to a boil. Add garlic and ginger; reduce heat and simmer for 10 minutes. Add pineapple, tomato, red pepper and cinnamon and simmer an additional 10 minutes or until tomato becomes incorporated into sauce. Remove from heat and set sauce aside.

Heat oil to 350° F (175° C) to fry pork. Toss marinated pork in flour and cornstarch mixture and fry in hot oil until cooked, about 5 minutes. Drain well on kitchen towel. Heat sauce through, adding snow peas just before serving. Spoon sauce over pork and serve with rice or noodles.

Tip
Try this dish with other meats, such as chicken or beef; it also works well with tofu. The sauce can be made up to 3 days ahead and stored in the fridge.

Silky Chicken Curry
Serves 6

The first immigrants from India were Sikhs who landed in Vancouver in 1904; they found work mostly in the timber industry. Despite institutionalized discrimination that lasted well into the century, Sikhs and other Indians continued to arrive in B.C. and make their contribution to our multicultural landscape. Over the past decade, Indian cuisine has become a major player on the B.C. food scene. Indian restaurants have evolved from obscurity to the point where people will now wait over two hours for a table at the city's top Indian restaurant, Vij's. This popularity is attributable not only to the character and complexity of the cuisine, but to B.C.'s huge ethnic population and love of unique cuisines.

¼ cup (60 mL) unsalted butter

3 medium onions, finely diced

3 cloves garlic, minced

1 Tbsp (15 mL) grated fresh ginger

⅓ cup (75 mL) curry paste

2 tsp (10 mL) freshly ground cumin

pinch of cayenne or chilies (optional)

2½ lbs (1.2 kg) diced chicken or a 4 lb (2 kg) chicken, cut into 10 pieces

2 medium carrots, peeled and diagonally sliced

1 red pepper, diced

1 medium tomato, diced

1 cup (250 mL) coconut milk

sea salt and freshly ground pepper

fresh cilantro, chopped

1 cup (250 mL) toasted and chopped unsalted cashews

Melt butter over medium heat in a wide, heavy-bottomed pot. Add onions, garlic and ginger and cook about 5 minutes. Stir in curry paste, cumin and cayenne and cook 2 minutes. Add chicken, stirring to coat, then add carrots, red pepper, tomato and coconut milk.

Bring to a simmer, cover and cook about 30 minutes, or until chicken is cooked. Season with salt and pepper. Curry can be made up to 3 days in advance and refrigerated.

Serve curry hot, garnished with cilantro and cashews, accompanied by basmati or jasmine rice and a side of plain yogurt or raita (see opposite).

Raita

Peel, seed and grate cucumbers into a colander and let drain 15 minutes. Transfer grated cucumber to a bowl, squeezing out as much moisture as possible, then stir in yogurt, mint, cumin, salt and pepper. Store, refrigerated, for up to 5 days.

2 long English cucumbers

1 cup (250 mL) plain yogurt

¼ cup (60 mL) fresh chopped mint

ground cumin, sea salt and freshly ground pepper to taste

Tip

If you are fearful of cooking rice (and don't have an electric rice cooker), try this foolproof method. Cook your rice as you would cook pasta, in a big pot of boiling salted water. Check rice often for doneness, then drain in a fine mesh colander and serve. This method is especially suited to cooking large quantities of rice.

Duck Confit with Caramelized Rutabaga and Risotto

Serves 10

Risotto is a traditional Italian dish that you can find in many of the province's finest restaurants (and not just Italian ones). This method of cooking rice uses a special variety of rice called Arborio (Carnaroli or Vialone Nano can also be used) that is "toasted" or sautéed in olive oil or butter before broth is added to the dish. The result is a very creamy rice that has a nice "al dente" bite to it when it is finished cooking. For this recipe we have chosen to incorporate one of our favourite fall vegetables, rutabagas. If you don't have time to make duck confit, you can buy it ready-made at Oyama Sausage. Duck confit is simply duck that has been salt cured and poached in its own fat until it is very tender.

10 duck legs

2 heads garlic, halved crosswise

1 lemon, sliced into about 5 rings

1 orange, sliced into about 5 rings

½ cinnamon stick

4 star anise, whole

1 tsp (5 mL) black peppercorns, whole

½ inch (1 cm) fresh ginger, sliced into three pieces

6 sprigs of fresh thyme

3 bay leaves

½ lb (250 g) kosher salt

about 2 lbs (1 kg) of rendered duck fat and 4 cups (1 L) grape seed or olive oil

Rutabaga

2 Tbsp (30 mL) butter

2 Tbsp (30 mL) brown sugar

2 small rutabaga, peeled, quartered and sliced, ¼ inch (.5 cm) thick

sea salt and freshly ground pepper to taste

Layer the duck legs, garlic halves, lemon and orange slices, spices and herbs, in a nonreactive container, generously sprinkling with salt between each layer. Cover with plastic wrap, and cure in refrigerator for 24 hours.

Preheat the oven to 250° F (120° C). Remove the duck legs and pat them dry (you can rinse them if you prefer a milder salt flavour). Rinse and drain garlic, fruit, spices and herbs. Place duck legs and fruit mixture, alternating layers, into a deep baking dish and cover with the duck fat and oil. Bake for 6 to 8 hours or until the meat is very tender. The duck is ready to serve hot or it can be cooled and preserved in a crock or plastic container in the refrigerator for up to 3 months. If storing, strain the fat through a fine sieve and pour enough over the meat to cover.

To prepare the rutabaga, heat butter and brown sugar in a small pan until butter is melted. Add rutabaga slices and cook over medium heat until tender, about 12 to 15 minutes. Season with salt and pepper and set aside.

For the risotto, melt butter in a skillet over medium heat and sauté onion until softened but not coloured, about 5 minutes. Add the rice and sauté for 2 to 4 minutes, stirring to coat the grains. Then add the white wine, stir to combine until it is absorbed, about 3 minutes. Add a ladle of the hot broth, stirring slowly but continuously, until it is almost completely absorbed by the rice. Continue adding broth until all of it is absorbed and the rice is tender but slightly chewy and very creamy. This will take about 25 minutes. Stir in the remaining tablespoon of butter, parsley and Parmesan cheese. Add salt and pepper to taste. Serve the risotto piping hot with the duck confit and caramelized rutabaga.

Risotto

¼ cup (60 mL) unsalted butter, plus 1 Tbsp to finish

¼ cup (60 mL) onion, chopped

2 cups (500 mL) Arborio rice

½ cup (125 mL) white wine

5 cups (1.25 L) hot chicken or vegetable broth

¼ cup (60 mL) parsley, chopped

½ cup (125 mL) Parmesan cheese, grated

sea salt and freshly ground pepper to taste

Coffee and Chocolate Braised Short Ribs

Serves 6

Short ribs have not always been the darling staple of top restaurants. This cut of meat has lots of fat, meat, bone and connective tissue and was once considered "what was left" after the choice cuts of beef were taken. However, some simple kitchen magic entailing trimming and a long, moist cooking method results in meat that is tender, rich and flavourful. There are lots of short rib recipes calling for a wine-based braising liquid, but because Vancouver has such a strong coffee culture, we felt some java would be an appropriate substitution. Use any good, strong coffee that is not too bitter and combine it with your favourite dark chocolate for a unique dish that will have your friends coming back for more!

¼ cup (60 mL) olive oil

5 lbs (2.3 kg) beef short ribs

sea salt and freshly ground pepper

1 large onion, chopped

1 large red pepper, chopped

1 large jalapeño pepper, seeded and finely chopped

4 garlic cloves, minced

2 Tbsp (30 mL) dark brown sugar

2 Tbsp (30 mL) ancho chile powder

¼ cup (60 mL) fresh oregano, chopped

1 tsp (5 mL) cumin

2 cups (500 mL) strong coffee

1 x 28 oz (796 mL) can diced tomatoes in juice

1 Tbsp (15 mL) tomato paste

1 cup (250 mL) dark, unsweetened chocolate, at least 70% cocoa, shaved

chopped fresh cilantro

Preheat oven to 300° F (150° C). Heat oil in a heavy-bottomed pot over medium-high heat. Season beef short ribs with salt and pepper. Working in batches, sear short ribs in oil until nicely browned and transfer to a platter.

Reduce heat to medium and add onions and peppers to the oil and drippings in the pot, stirring until onions are translucent. Stir in garlic and sauté for 1 minute. Add brown sugar, ancho chile powder, oregano, and cumin and cook for 5 minutes. Stir in coffee, tomatoes, tomato paste and bring the mixture to a boil. Add the short ribs and the collected juices to the pot and heat until boiling.

Cover and bake in oven until the meat is very tender, about 1¾ to 2 hours. Stir in chocolate until it is melted and evenly distributed in the sauce. Season to taste with salt and pepper and garnish with cilantro. Serve with Smashed Pemberton Fingerlings with Fresh Herbs and Truffle Oil (see p. 108).

Pappardelle with Black Winter Truffles

Serves 4

While not specifically B.C., the truffle is enjoying a resurgence in cooking with many of B.C.'s top regional chefs using it to enhance local ingredients and dishes. Often called "the perfume of the earth itself," the truffle is a coveted aphrodisiac, strongly scented with a musky earthiness that is evocative of sex and mystery. Most truffles are harvested in late fall or winter and you can find fresh truffles at specialty markets across the province, but they will cost you a pretty penny—they run anywhere from $700 to $3000 dollars per pound (half kilogram). If you are more budget conscious, you can more easily find truffle butter, versatile truffle oil or even truffle salt, giving you the pleasure of the flavour at a more reasonable cost. And you can use that truffle oil for tons of dishes from truffle fries to popcorn!

Cream Sauce

1 Tbsp (15 mL) butter

¼ cup (60 mL) onion, finely chopped

½ cup (125 mL) white wine

½ cup (125 mL) heavy cream (32%)

sea salt and freshly ground pepper

¼ cup (60 mL) grated Parmesan cheese

1 lb (500 g) fresh pappardelle, homemade (see next page) or store-bought

1 medium black winter truffle, grated, sliced or shaved

Melt butter in a skillet and sauté onion until soft. Add white wine and simmer until half the liquid is reduced. Stir in cream and simmer for 5 minutes. Season with salt and pepper.

Bring a large pot of salted water to a boil, add the pappardelle and cook until al dente, for about 5 minutes. Drain and transfer pasta to the skillet with the cream sauce and add Parmesan cheese. Toss gently to mix and transfer to a warm serving bowl. Grate fresh truffle over pasta and serve.

Tip

Have a pot of boiling water ready first, and you can prepare the sauce and cook the pasta at the same time.

Homemade Pasta

Mix flour and eggs on low speed in a heavy-duty electric mixer until mixture has a coarse, crumbly look, like corn meal. Add water in small quantities until the mixture starts to hold together. Switch to the dough hook on the mixer, or knead by hand 7 to 10 minutes. Dough should not be sticky or in separate pieces. Add a little more liquid if needed, or a little more flour if sticky. Cover with plastic wrap and let dough rest 15 to 30 minutes. Roll through a pasta machine according to the manufacturer's instructions.

To cook, make sure water is at a full boil and very well salted. Fresh pasta cooks very quickly and will rise to the top of the water when done. Drain in a colander and do not rinse.

1½ cups (375 mL) semolina flour

2 eggs

2 to 3 tsp (10 to 15 mL) lukewarm water

Birch Syrup Roasted Squash Ravioli with Brown Butter Hazelnut Sauce

Serves

Birch syrup is one of B.C.'s best-kept secrets. Like maple syrup, birch syrup is made using the reduced sap from its mother tree. However, the main difference between birch and maple syrup is that it takes double the amount of sap from a birch tree to make the same amount of syrup; incredibly, this means 85 to 105 quarts (80 to 100 L) of sap must be collected to make 1 quart (1 L) of syrup! As a result, birch syrup is nearly five times the price of maple syrup. Don't let this deter you from splurging on this unique syrup from Northern B.C. to complement Similkameen Valley squash and Fraser Valley hazelnuts for a truly British Columbian fall dish.

½ cup (125 mL) unsalted butter

½ small onion, diced

1 cup (250 mL) roasted butternut squash purée

sea salt and freshly ground pepper to taste

3 Tbsp (45 mL) heavy cream (32%)

3 Tbsp (45 mL) grated Parmesan cheese, plus more for topping

pinch of nutmeg

1 recipe pasta dough, rolled out into wide ribbons

½ cup (125 mL) roughly chopped hazelnuts

1 Tbsp (15 mL) finely chopped fresh parsley leaves

In a large pan, melt 1 Tbsp (15 mL) of butter and sauté onions over medium heat. Add the butternut squash purée and cook until the mixture is slightly dry, about 2 to 3 minutes. Season with salt and pepper. Stir in cream and continue to cook for 2 minutes. Remove from the heat and stir in Parmesan cheese and nutmeg, and season with salt and pepper. Set the filling aside to cool completely.

For pasta recipe, please see p. 105.

Set a large pot of salted water to boil. Cut the pasta ribbons into 3-inch (7.5 cm) squares. Place 2 tsp (10 mL) of the filling in the centre of each ravioli square. Using a pastry brush, lightly brush the edges of the pasta with water and cover with a second square. Press edges slightly to seal. If desired, you can cut the pasta into circles with a round cookie cutter. Add the ravioli to pot of boiling water and cook until al dente, about 2 to 3 minutes, or until they are paler in colour and float to the surface. With a slotted spoon, remove the ravioli from the water and drain well.

In a large pan, melt the remaining butter over medium-high heat, add the hazelnuts and continue to cook until the butter starts to brown. Remove from the heat and toss ravioli in butter.

Place ravioli in the centre of each serving plate and spoon any remaining butter sauce and hazelnuts on top. Sprinkle Parmesan cheese over the pasta and garnish with parsley.

Birch Syrup Butternut Squash Purée

Preheat oven to 375° F (190° C). Cut one butternut squash in half lengthwise, scoop out seeds and place flesh side up on a baking pan. Pour birch syrup on top, season lightly with salt and pepper and bake in oven for 45 minutes or until tender when pierced with a fork. Cool, scoop out flesh and mash.

Birch Syrup Buttenut Squash Purée

1 x 1 lb (500g) butternut squash

⅓ cup (75 mL) birch syrup

sea salt and fresh ground pepper

Smashed Pemberton Fingerlings with Fresh Herbs and Truffle Oil

Serves 6

Combining two great earthy ingredients—Pemberton fingerling potatoes and aromatic truffle oil—makes for a heavenly combination of flavours. Truffle oil is made by infusing good quality oil (usually olive), with luxurious Italian white or black truffles. The oil absorbs the aroma and flavour of the pungent fungi and turns ordinary smashed potatoes into something that tastes elegantly divine. And don't just use truffle oil for potatoes, try it with B.C. free-range eggs, Okanagan goat cheese or even local Chilliwack popping corn!

2 lbs (1 kg) fingerling potatoes

¼ cup (60 mL) butter, sliced

3 Tbsp (45 mL) heavy cream (32%)

⅓ cup (75 mL) sour cream

sea salt and freshly ground pepper to taste

¼ cup (60 mL) fresh herbs (use some of your favourites, such as thyme, rosemary, tarragon or dill)

truffle oil for drizzling

In a large pot, cover potatoes with salted water and bring to a boil over high heat. Reduce to medium-high heat and cook until the potatoes are tender when pricked with a fork, about 15 minutes. Drain, and return potatoes to pot.

Add butter and whipping cream to the potatoes, and smash potatoes into uneven chunks with a large fork or potato masher. Mix in sour cream and fresh herbs, and season with salt and pepper. Drizzle truffle oil on top of the potatoes and serve.

Roasted Jerusalem Artichokes

Serves 4

Also known as "sunchokes" and "Canada's potatoes," Jerusalem artichokes are easy to grow here and will even produce a display of small sunflowers late in the summer. In B.C., Jerusalem artichokes are best harvested in the fall when light frosts enhance their natural sweetness. A tuber native to North America, the Jerusalem artichoke's waxy flesh has the texture of a crispy apple and a flavour reminiscent of sunflower seeds. Traditionally, the tubers were simply boiled and eaten much like potatoes, and they can be used in place of potatoes in many recipes. They also make excellent soups!

4 cloves garlic, chopped

2½ Tbsp (37 mL) extra virgin olive oil

1½ lbs (750 g) Jerusalem artichokes

sea salt and freshly ground black pepper to taste

1 Tbsp (15 mL) chopped fresh parsley

Preheat oven to 350° F (175° C). Heat garlic and oil in a small pot and cook until soft. Peel Jerusalem artichokes and cut into small chunks, placing chunks into a bowl of acidulated water (see next page) as you work. Put in a shallow roasting pan large enough to hold everything in one layer comfortably. Strain garlic from oil and pour oil over the chokes. Add salt and pepper and toss.

Bake in oven for about 20 minutes, stirring once or twice, until tender. Sprinkle parsley on top and serve as a side dish.

The Jerusalem artichoke has no ties to the famous Biblical city; the name simply comes from the English misunderstanding of the Italian word girasol, which means "sunflower."

Acidulated water is just water to which a little acid—normally lemon or lime juice or vinegar—has been added; ½ tsp (2 mL) per cup (250 mL) is enough. When you are peeling or cutting fruits or vegetables that discolour quickly when exposed to air, like apples, place them in acidulated water to prevent browning. Jerusalem artichokes, globe artichokes and salsify are just some of the foods that benefit from this treatment. Acidulated water is also sometimes used for cooking.

Brussels Sprouts with Pancetta and Pine Nuts

Serves 6

Because they do well in cool climates, Brussels sprouts are perfectly suited to B.C.; they even improve in flavour, sweetness and tenderness if allowed to chill through the first few frosts. Brussels sprouts came originally from the region around Afghanistan and, like cauliflower, are actually a variety of cabbage. Because Brussels sprouts are often overcooked, they do not hold a place among the stars of the vegetable kingdom (nor at many dinner tables), which is a shame. Try this recipe with goose proscuitto or even proscuitto "bits" from Oyama Sausage at Granville Island. They take extra special care when raising their pork, even going so far as to feed the hogs organic hazelnuts to try to incorporate better flavour in the meat, from the inside out!

2 lbs (1 kg) Brussels sprouts

splash of olive oil

5 oz (140 g) pancetta or proscuitto, diced

sea salt and freshly ground pepper to taste

½ cup (125 mL) pine nuts, toasted

Preheat oven to 400° F (200° C). Slice the Brussels sprouts in half lengthwise, removing any loose, outer leaves and trimming the bottom stems. Toss in olive oil and add pancetta or proscuitto, salt and pepper. Spread in a single layer on a baking sheet and bake for 20 to 30 minutes until pancetta or proscuitto is crispy. Stir occasionally, so the Brussels sprouts cook evenly. Toss with the pine nuts and another splash of olive oil, if desired.

Tip
To toast pine nuts, place in a dry frying pan and cook on low heat, stirring occasionally, until lightly golden.

Pancetta is Italian bacon. Proscuitto is a type of Italian dry-cured meat, usually made from pork.

Candied Yams

Serves 4 to 6

This recipe is usually made for Thanksgiving or other celebrations, but it is actually a quick and simple dish to make anytime. The yam is one of the oldest vegetables commonly used today; it is native to Africa and Asia and has been cultivated possibly as far back as 8000 BC. Most of the major yam-growing countries are still in Africa, Nigeria being the top producer. The yam is often confused with the sweet potato, a vegetable with its own ancient history, native to the tropical areas of the Americas and likely in cultivation 5000 years ago. The yam is a member of the lily family while the sweet potato is a member of the magnolia family. Although both are used like potatoes, they are both only distantly related to that tuber.

1 cup (250 mL) birch syrup

1 cup (250 mL) orange juice

½ cup (125 mL) fresh lime juice

½ cup (125 mL) water

¼ cup (60 mL) melted butter

3 lbs (1.5 kg) yams

Combine birch syrup, fruit juices and water in a nonreactive saucepan large enough to hold all the sweet potatoes comfortably. Bring to a boil, then reduce to a simmer.

Peel the yams, slicing the longer ones in half, and place in the saucepan. Cook, turning occasionally, for about 1½ hours, or until the edges of the yams turn slightly translucent and they are tender.

Transfer onto a serving platter and drizzle with the melted butter.

Yams contain more natural sugar than sweet potatoes and have a higher moisture content.

Oven-roasted Quince

Serves 4

Quince is a wonderful but little-known fruit in B.C. Known as "the golden apple," it is native to Persia and Greece, although it was the Greeks who first cultivated this fruit as we know it today. Many historical accounts of the apple are likely botanical cases of mistaken identity that actually refer to the quince. Quince grown in northern climates is inedible when raw because it is too sour and hard; however, once cooked whole or made into a paste, this fruit can be used in sauces, as an accompaniment to roasted meats or eaten like applesauce.

2 large quince, peeled and halved

2 cups (500 mL) honey

2 cups (500 mL) water

½ cup (125 mL) orange juice

1 vanilla bean, halved and split

Cinnamon Ice Cream

2 cups (500 mL) best quality vanilla ice cream

2 Tbsp (30 mL) ground cinnamon

Preheat oven to 275° F (135° C). Combine all ingredients in an ovenproof dish and bring to a boil on the stovetop. Cover with a piece of parchment paper and weigh down with a small plate. Bake in oven for 3 hours, turning once during cooking.

Remove from oven and let cool. Store quince refrigerated in the syrup for up to 6 months.

To serve, pour syrup into a small pot and reduce it until it becomes a deep red, then toss the quince in the syrup to coat. Serve with Cinnamon Ice Cream.

Cinnamon Ice Cream
In an electric mixer or food processor, combine ice cream with cinnamon.

Mix to combine, then freeze until set.

Vanilla beans can used to infuse sugar with its wonderful aroma and flavour. Cut a vanilla bean in half lengthwise (or dry and reuse the pods from the recipe) and cover with 1 to 2 cups (250 to 500 ml) of white sugar for 3 to 4 weeks or more, stirring once a week. You can use vanilla sugar in your coffee or tea, or add it to whipped cream.

Creamy Espresso Martini

Serves 1

A perfect Vancouver day (rain or shine) always involves outdoor activity on one of our mountains, at the beach or in Stanley Park and a coffee-based drink. With a coffee house (or two) on almost every city block, Vancouverites love their grande, non-fat, extra-hot, double-shot, half-sweet, extra-foam lattes. This recipe takes our early morning habit and turns it into a delectable evening treat. For this recipe, try using a local house blend such as that from Café Artigiano, where the staff and owners continually garner awards as some of the best baristas in the world!

1 oz (30 mL) cold espresso

1½ oz (45 mL) vodka, coffee or vanilla flavour

1½ oz (45 mL) coffee liqueur

1 oz (30 mL) Irish cream liqueur

1 scoop (¼ cup [60 mL]) vanilla ice cream

Pour ingredients into a shaker and shake vigorously. Strain into a chilled martini glass.

Coffee is the most popular beverage worldwide. But did you know that most people employed to grow and harvest coffee beans live well below the poverty line and are not paid a fair price for their labour? Considering the multi-billion dollar profit the coffee industry boasts, we recommend you seek out and purchase Fair Trade and organically grown coffee so that you may enjoy your java guilt-free.

Caramel-dipped Apples

Serves 8

This recipe is inspired by summer memories of the Pacific National Exhibition (PNE), which takes places the last two weeks of August every year in Vancouver. The PNE has been a Vancouver tradition since 1910 when it was founded, and it now welcomes more than three million people every year. For many families in B.C., the fair is a tradition, and each person must stop at his or her favourite food court stand, whether it be the mini-donuts, whales tails, cotton candy or caramel apples. The next time you are craving a taste of summer and you can't make it to the PNE, try this recipe.

1 lb (500 g) dark brown sugar

¾ cup (175 mL) unsalted butter, room temperature

1 x 10 oz (300 mL) can sweetened condensed milk

⅔ cup (150 mL) light corn syrup

¼ tsp (1 mL) sea salt

1 tsp (5 mL) vanilla

¼ cup (60 mL) heavy cream (32%)

8 apples, such as Macintosh or Granny Smith, stems removed, washed and dried

8 wooden sticks such as craft sticks, popsicle sticks or even chopsticks

Combine brown sugar, butter, condensed milk, corn syrup and salt in a heavy-bottomed pot over medium-low heat and stir slowly but continually to dissolve sugar until it reaches a temperature between 234° F and 240° F (112° C and 115° C) on a candy thermometer, or the soft-ball stage (see opposite). Remove from heat, stir in vanilla and whipping cream and pour into a clean metal bowl. Cool until caramel is 200° F (95° C), about 15 minutes.

While caramel is cooling, line a baking sheet with buttered parchment paper and push a stick into the stem end of each apple. Dip apples in caramel and let excess caramel drip off before setting on the greased paper. Cool before eating. Chill any uneaten apples, wrapped in cellophane, up to 1 week.

Tip
If your apples are quite waxy, dip them in boiling water for 30 seconds to remove the wax, and dry very well.

Tip
Once the caramel apples have set, dip them into melted chocolate for an extra decadent Halloween treat. You can also roll them in chopped nuts, candy sprinkles or crushed candy bars!

Tip
The soft-ball stage is a candy test where you drop a little syrup in cold water, and as the syrup cools, it forms a soft ball that flattens when it is removed from the water.

Cucumber and Fresh Dill Salad

Serves 6

Cucumbers in B.C. are typically grown in greenhouses all year, with the possibility of achieving 2 or even 3 growing cycles. However, many people prefer to wait for the warmer summer months to enjoy the farm-fresh, field-grown cucumbers that are perfect for this salad. They are full of flavour, but you do have to remember to seed them. The addition of fresh dill to this salad almost gives the illusion of tasting a dill pickle, but with a much fresher taste. And remember, cucumbers are comprised mostly of water, which quickly gets released into the dressing, so it is best to serve this salad as soon as it's made.

4 large, long English cucumbers

1 medium red onion, halved and thinly sliced

1 bunch fresh dill, finely chopped, about 1 cup (250 mL)

¼ cup (60 mL) cider vinegar

1 to 2 Tbsp (15 to 30 mL) honey, to taste

1 cup (250 ml) sour cream or plain yogurt

sea salt and freshly ground pepper to taste

Wash the cucumbers and peel in lengthwise strips, being sure to leave a bit of dark green skin between each strip. Thinly slice, and place slices, along with the onion and fresh dill, in a large glass bowl.

A mature cucumber plant can use 4 to 5L of water per day.

In a separate, small bowl, make a dressing with the vinegar, honey, sour cream, salt and pepper. Add dressing to large bowl and mix well to combine.

Allow the salad to sit for at least 15 minutes before serving as a side dish.

Although considered a vegetable, cucumbers are actually the fruit of the cucumber plant, which belongs to the same family of plants as melons and pumpkins.

Grilled Asian Pears and Avocado Salad with Lemongrass and Garam Masala Vinaigrette

Serves 4

At one time, Asian or Indian food ingredients were only available in specialty ethnic markets. Now, with the rising popularity of ethnic cuisine and the proliferation of multi-ethnic communities in B.C., these once hard-to-find ingredients are available in local grocery stores throughout the province. This recipe combines both Asian and Indian flavours to create a mouth-watering salad using the fresh citrus flavour of lemon grass and the heady aroma of garam masala. Although we prefer to use Vij's own blend of the spice, which you can purchase at his restaurant or at other gourmet retailers in Vancouver, any blend will work fine. The other secret to this recipe is the grilled avocado—once you have tried this, you will never eat an ungrilled avocado again.

¼ cup (60 mL) canola oil

2 Tbsp (30 mL) honey

2 Asian pears, halved

2 avocados, peeled, halved and cut into 4 slices

½ lb (250 g) baby salad greens

sea salt and freshly ground pepper

Garam Masala Vinaigrette

¼ cup (60 mL) garam masala paste

⅓ cup (75 mL) oil

¼ cup (60 mL) rice wine vinegar

Mix oil and honey together in a small bowl. Brush on Asian pears and avocados and grill over medium heat for about 5 minutes. Season with salt and pepper.

For the vinaigrette, whisk the garam masala paste, oil and rice wine vinegar together in a small bowl. Add the vinaigrette to the salad greens and serve on individual plates with the pears and avocado.

Potato and Roasted Garlic Chowder

Serves 4

Garlic has long been reputed to prevent everything from the common cold and flu to the plague. Besides this, it makes almost everything taste good—including ordinary potato chowder. Roasting whole garlic neutralizes its pungency and brings out its sweetness; local B.C. potatoes are a perfect foil to its mellow flavour. Delicious and nutritious, this soup is sure to ward off the usual wintertime ailments. Stop by your local winter farmer's market and find some Okanagan or Similkameen Valley garlic, with large bulbs that are perfect for roasting.

2 medium onions, diced

¼ cup (60 mL) unsalted butter

1 Tbsp (15 mL) olive oil

2 cups (500 mL) celery, diced

1 cup (250 mL) carrots, diced

4 medium potatoes, peeled and diced

1 bay leaf

vegetable or chicken stock, enough to just cover vegetables

2 bulbs roasted garlic (see next page), cloves squeezed out and roughly chopped

2 cups (500 ml) heavy cream (32%)

sea salt and freshly ground pepper to taste

¼ cup (60 ml) fresh herbs such as parsley, thyme or mint, chopped

In a heavy pot, sauté the onions in the butter and oil until they turn golden. Add the vegetables, bay leaf and cover with stock. Simmer for 15 minutes, then add the roasted garlic and cream, and simmer for 10 to 15 minutes more or until the potatoes are cooked and the soup is reduced and creamy. Season to taste with salt and pepper. Ladle soup into bowls and garnish with a sprinkle of herbs.

Roasted Garlic

You can roast as little or as much garlic as you want. I tend to roast 5 or 6 bulbs at a time, so I will have leftovers to last a week. Preheat the oven to 350° F (175° C). Slice the top of each bulb of garlic to expose the cloves, and lay them cut side up in a baking dish. Drizzle with olive oil and sprinkle with sea salt. Roast 20 to 30 minutes or until cloves are tender. Remove from oven and set aside until cool enough to handle. The buttery flesh of the cloves will come out of the bulb easily when you squeeze it (throw out the papery skin of the bulb). Alternatively, you can serve the whole roasted bulbs as a garnish to grilled meats or vegetables.

Kitsilano Maple Cream Ale and Cheddar Soup

Serves 4

It doesn't get more Canadian than maple syrup, beer and cheddar cheese. Beer and maple syrup? This interesting flavour combination is uniquely West Coast, thanks to Granville Island Brewing, which opened its doors in 1984 as one of Canada's first microbreweries and continues today as a leader in B.C.'s microbrew industry. One of its most popular beers to date is the Kitsilano Maple Cream Ale, which combines pure Canadian maple syrup with its traditional hand-crafted beer. There is no better beer for this hearty winter soup, featuring another Canadian favourite: cheddar cheese.

2 medium onions, diced

1 Tbsp (15 ml) olive oil

¼ cup (60 ml) unsalted butter

2 cups (500 ml) celery, diced

1 cup (250 ml) parsnips, diced

4 medium potatoes, peeled and diced

1 bay leaf

vegetable or chicken stock, enough to just cover vegetables

2 cups (500 ml) heavy cream (32%)

2 cups (500 ml) sharp white Cheddar cheese, grated

½ to 1 bottle of Kitsilano Maple Cream Ale, about 6 to 12 oz (170 to 341 mL) or to taste

sea salt and freshly ground pepper

In a heavy pot, sauté the onions in the butter and oil until they turn golden. Add celery, parsnips, potatoes, bay leaf and add enough stock to cover everything. Simmer for 15 minutes, then add the cream and simmer for 10 to 15 minutes more or until the potatoes are cooked and the soup is reduced and creamy. Remove soup from heat and blend in cheese in small batches. Puree soup in a blender and return to medium-low heat and stir in ale to taste. Season with salt and pepper and serve.

Canadians spend over 6.7 billion dollars per year on beer, accounting for more than 51 percent of the sales of all alcohol combined.

Cioppino with Fennel and Saffron

Serves 6

Cioppino is an Italian seafood stew whose North American roots are thought to have originated in the San Francisco Bay area when Italian immigrants from Genoa replaced traditional Genoese ingredients with the fresh fish available to them on the West Coast. Most Italians who came to Canada before World War II came by way of the United States and brought with them this cioppino. The combination of B.C.'s abundance of fresh, local seafood and the large Italian district of Commercial Drive, located on the east side of Vancouver, means that a good bowl of cioppino is not hard to find; just be sure to ask for a bib because it can be a deliciously messy experience!

2 lbs (1 kg) snapper fillet, cleaned

1 lb (500 g) fresh shrimp, tails on

½ lb (250 g) each clams, mussels and scallops

1 crab, cooked, cleaned and cracked

2 Tbsp (30 mL) extra virgin olive oil

1 small onion, minced

1 medium fennel bulb, diced

1 cup (250 mL) white wine

3 cloves garlic, minced

zest from half an orange, minced

pinch of saffron, or to taste, dissolved in ¼ cup (60 mL) warm stock

4 cups (1 L) tomato sauce

3 cups (750 mL) fish stock

sea salt and freshly ground pepper

½ cup (125 mL) fresh basil for garnish

Wash all fish and seafood, except crab, and pat dry. In a heavy-bottomed pot, heat oil and sauté onion. Stir in fennel and sauté for 5 minutes. Add wine and garlic, and simmer for 10 minutes. Stir in orange zest, saffron, tomato sauce and stock, and simmer for 10 minutes. Nestle fish fillets and seafood into the sauce, making sure to cover them with liquid. Cover, bring back to a simmer over medium-high heat and cook until clams and mussels open, about 10 to 12 minutes. Season with salt and pepper. Serve hot in warmed bowls, garnished with fresh basil.

Tip
It is traditional to serve cioppino with polenta and a bottle of Chianti.

Note
If you have trouble finding polenta and mascarpone, try an Italian deli.

Polenta with Mascarpone

Bring milk and cream to a boil. Whisk in polenta and cook, stirring continuously, for 20 minutes. Season to taste with salt and pepper. Serve hot topped with mascarpone. You can also pour polenta into a rectangular baking dish. Once cooled, it can be sliced and pan-grilled with butter.

4 cups (1 L) milk
½ cup (125 mL) heavy cream (32%)
1 cup (250 mL) polenta
sea salt and freshly ground pepper to taste
1 cup (250 mL) mascarpone

Caramelized Onion and Goat Cheese Tart

Serves 6

Goats are year-round milk producers, which means that any season is goat cheese season in B.C.! Luckily for us, we have a number of talented artisan goat cheese producers, such as David Wood at Salt Spring Island Cheese Company or Carmelis in the Okanagan, who capitalize on this availability and are making some really fabulous cheeses. You can't go wrong with sweet caramelized onions and savoury goat cheese in this tart—perfect for brunch or a light dinner.

1 Tbsp (15 mL) oil

1 Tbsp (15 mL butter

6 medium yellow onions, thinly sliced

sea salt to taste

1 tsp (5 mL) sugar

1 Tbsp (15 mL) balsamic vinegar

Béchamel

2 Tbsp (30 mL) butter

2 Tbsp (30 mL) flour

1 cup (250 mL) milk

1 bay leaf

pinch of nutmeg

1 x ¾ lb (397 g) package frozen puff pastry, thawed

egg wash made with 1 beaten egg and a splash of water

8 oz (250 g) goat cheese

2 Tbsp (30 mL) chopped fresh herbs, such as parsley, thyme or sage (optional)

Heat oil and butter in a large pan over medium heat. Add the onions, season with salt and cook until softened, about 6 minutes. Stir in the sugar and balsamic vinegar, turn the heat to medium low and cook for 30 to 45 minutes, stirring often, until nicely caramelized.

To make the béchamel, melt the butter in a small, heavy saucepan over low heat. Add flour into melted butter and stir over low heat for 5 to 7 minutes. Slowly add milk, bay leaf and nutmeg, stirring constantly, and cook for about 10 more minutes until smooth and thick.

Preheat oven to 400° F (200° C). Roll out the pastry to ⅛ inch (.25 cm) thick and place on a rectangular baking sheet. Prick all over with a fork. Brush the outside edges, about ½ inch (1 cm), with egg wash.

Combine onions and béchamel sauce in a bowl. Crumble in goat cheese and fresh herbs, if desired, and stir to combine.

Spread onion mixture onto pastry and bake for 15 to 20 minutes until pastry is puffed and golden. Let sit 10 minutes before cutting into squares. Serve warm or at room temperature with a lightly dressed green salad and port sauce (see opposite).

In a small saucepan, combine port and stock and reduce over medium heat until thick and syrupy.

Tip
This tart is perfect for picnics, potlucks and lazy Sunday brunches. Best served at room temperature or slightly warm, it makes a great "do ahead" choice for travelling or entertaining. It also could be done in individual tart shells for easy serving.

Port Sauce
1 cup (250 mL) port
½ cup (125 mL) chicken stock

White Wine and Garlic Mussels

Serves 4 to 6

Fresh mussels steamed in white wine is a natural B.C. dish, but local mussels are hard to come by because they are also a favourite delicacy of ducks, raccoons and even starfish! If you get an opportunity, try to find B.C. Honey or Gallo Mussels, which are harvested in places such as Redonda, Salt Spring and Cortes Islands. These mussels are large and have rich, plump meat. However, due to their rarity, you will usually only find them on restaurant menus, and even then only as an appetizer portion due to their high price. B.C. only began seriously cultivating mussels in 1999, so this young industry will surely grow in the coming years.

4 lbs (2 kg) mussels

1 cup (250 mL) white wine such as Chardonnay

4 garlic cloves, minced

1 Tbsp (15 mL) butter

¼ cup (60 mL) chives, chopped

Scrub mussels under cool running water and remove any beards. Discard mussels that don't close when gently tapped.

Place white wine and garlic in a large pot and bring to a boil. Add mussels to the pot, cover and reduce heat, cooking for about 5 to 6 minutes. Discard any mussels that have not opened. With a slotted spoon transfer the mussels into serving dishes.

Turn heat to high and bring the remaining liquid to a boil. Cook for 2 to 3 minutes, until it has reduced slightly, and whisk in butter. Spoon the sauce over mussels, sprinkle with chives and serve hot.

Tip

Use your fresh mussels within 24 hours of purchasing them. The best way to store fresh mussels is to put them in a colander and place the colander into a bowl. Cover the mussels with ice and then with a damp towel. The mussels will stay very cold and have good air circulation, without being submerged (or drowned) in water.

Blackened Trout with Oven-dried Tomatoes

Serves 2

A favourite pastime for many B.C. residents during the warmer months of the year is heading out to fish on one of the many lakes that dot the province. Nothing tastes better than a breakfast of pan-fried trout with brown butter and some eggs cooked over an open fire. However, for those winter evenings when you are in the comfort of your own home, many local fishmongers sell excellent farm-raised trout that will bring back those summer memories. The blackening spices in this recipe will warm you up and the oven-dried tomatoes are a hearty version of the sweet, vine-ripened, summer variety. You can even plan ahead next summer and dry your own heirloom tomatoes for recipes such as this.

2 lbs (1 kg) Roma tomatoes, halved lengthwise

3 cloves garlic, minced

¼ cup (60 mL) fresh thyme, chopped

sea salt and freshly ground black pepper to taste

½ cup (125 mL) extra virgin olive oil

Spice Mixture

2 tsp (10 mL) paprika

2 tsp (10 mL) chipotle powder or chili powder

2 tsp (10 mL) ground cumin

2 tsp (10 mL) dried thyme

1 tsp (5 mL) freshly ground black pepper

1 tsp (5 mL) sea salt

2 fresh trout, gutted but whole

2 Tbsp (30 mL) canola oil

Preheat the oven to 250 F (120° C).

Scoop out seeds from the tomatoes. Mix the garlic with the thyme, salt and pepper and olive oil. Place the tomatoes cut side up in a roasting pan and drizzle with the garlic mixture. Bake for at least 3 hours or until the tomatoes are dehydrated but still chewy.

Mix all the spices together in a bowl.

Rinse trout with water and pat dry with paper towels. Brush oil on the trout and rub it all over with the spice mixture.

Heat oil in a heavy-bottomed skillet until it is smoking hot. Place the prepared trout in the skillet and cook for 2 to 4 minutes and turn over. Cook until the fish is firm and cooked through, 3 to 4 minutes. To test doneness, the fish should flake easily with a fork but should not be dry. Serve with oven-dried tomatoes on the side.

Tip

Oven-drying tomatoes is a great way to preserve these tasty bits of summer sunshine. Grow tomatoes in your garden or in containers, or pick them up at farmers' markets.

Tip

Any leftover tomatoes can be covered in olive oil and stored in a jar. They will keep for up to 3 weeks refrigerated.

Sloping Hill Farm Hazelnut-roasted Pork with Birch Syrup

Serves 8 to 10

There are more than 175 pork producers in B.C. who raise more than 300,000 pigs annually, 90% of which are consumed within the province. This is in sharp contrast to 30 million pigs per year raised in Canada, which is the world's largest pork exporter—50% of our pork is exported to over 85 countries. Specialty farmers such as Sloping Hill Farm on Vancouver Island are raising the bar for locally produced organic pork by using free-range pens, limiting the number of animals and encouraging natural behavior. By using local pork, hazelnuts and birch syrup, this recipe is truly a testament to the best of the province.

Stuffing

2 Tbsp (30 mL) olive oil

1 onion, finely chopped

4 cloves garlic, roughly chopped

¼ cup (60 mL) fresh rosemary, chopped

¼ cup (60 mL) fresh thyme, chopped

2 cups (500 mL) hazelnuts, roughly chopped

¼ cup (60 mL) chicken stock

2 Tbsp (30 mL) dry bread crumbs

1 Tbsp (15 mL) dark brown sugar

2 x 3 lb (1.4 kg) pork loin rib roast, patted dry, room temperature

sea salt and freshly ground pepper

butcher twine

3 to 6 sprigs of fresh rosemary

1 Tbsp olive oil

Glaze

½ cup (125 mL) birch syrup

¼ cup (60 mL) white wine, preferably a Riesling

¼ cup (60 mL) chicken broth

sea salt and freshly ground pepper

Preheat oven to 400° F (200° C). Heat olive oil in a pan and cook onions, garlic, rosemary and thyme a few minutes. Add hazelnuts. Stir in chicken stock, bread crumbs and brown sugar, and set stuffing aside.

Turn the pork loin rib roast fat side down. Slit lengthwise, almost but not quite all the way through, to form a long pocket, leaving a ½ inch (1 cm) border of uncut meat at each end. Sprinkle generously with salt and pepper. Fill the cavity with the stuffing. Tie loin together with butcher twine or heavy duty kitchen string at 1½ inch (3 to 4 cm) intervals. Slide the rosemary sprigs under the twine. Brush with remaining olive oil and sprinkle generously with salt and pepper. Set, fat side up, diagonally or curved (so it fits) on a large baking sheet or jelly roll pan.

Mix birch syrup, white wine and chicken broth together. Brush glaze mixture on meat.

Roast in the oven until a meat thermometer registers 150° to 155° F (65° to 68° C), about 2 hours, occasionally brushing with the pan drippings. Let roast rest 15 to 20 minutes out of the oven, then transfer to a carving board.

To make the sauce, stir juices around pan to loosen browned bits. Pour through a strainer into a small pan, and stir in port and chicken stock. Bring to simmer and cook until lightly thickened. Slice pork roast and serve with sauce.

Sauce
¼ **cup (60 mL) port**
¼ **cup (60 mL) chicken stock**

Grilled Quail with Pistachio and Pomegranate

Serves 4

Quail belongs to a family of game birds that were vital to the survival of both native peoples and early settlers. You can see quail both in the wild and on signage for local businesses throughout the province's Okanagan region. While you may see many of these birds running across the roads, most of B.C.'s game birds used for food consumption are raised in captivity. Known for their rich, moist meat, quail are the most popular of the small-game birds, with more than 350,000 being produced annually. Other game birds being raised include pheasants, partridge, squab and silkies. While quail are frequently offered on the menus of upscale restaurants, they are also available for the home cook in specialty shops and meat markets.

4 quail, cut through back-bone and flattened out

sea salt and freshly ground pepper

Marinade

½ **garlic clove, minced**

1 **tsp (5 mL) cinnamon**

1 **tsp (5 mL) cumin**

½ **onion, finely chopped**

3 **Tbsp (45 mL) pomegranate molasses**

juice from half a lime

Sauce

1 **cup (250 mL) bacon, diced**

½ **garlic clove, minced**

¼ **cup (60 mL) pomegranate molasses**

½ **cup (125 mL) pistachios, whole**

sea salt and freshly ground pepper to taste

Garnish

Arugula leaves

In a large bowl, prepare marinade and toss to combine. Season each quail with salt and pepper and place in marinade. Cover and refrigerate for at least 1 hour and up to 24 hours.

For the sauce, sauté bacon in a pan until crispy. Remove all the fat drippings except for 1 Tbsp (15 mL). Add remaining ingredients and heat through.

Grill quail over medium-high heat for about 7 minutes each side, or until juices run clear.

Serve on a bed of arugula leaves with sauce drizzled on top.

Pomegranate molasses is a syrup made from cooked-down pomegranate juice. It can be found in Middle Eastern stores.

Tempura

Batter-laced deep-frying is a method of cooking that was introduced to Japan by Portuguese missionaries during the 16th century. By the 17th century, Tokyo street vendors were selling tempura, using fish freshly caught in Tokyo Bay and most often fried in sesame oil. This traditional cooking method has caught on in B.C. due to the huge interest in Japanese cuisine. It is now more common to have sushi days in elementary schools than hot dog days! This is a simple recipe that will please every member of your family. Be sure to choose the freshest possible ingredients, such as B.C. spot prawns, salmon, squash and even zucchini blossoms.

peanut oil

1 egg, beaten

1 cup (250 mL) cold beer

2 Tbsp (30 mL) dry white wine

½ cup (125 mL) flour

¼ cup (60 mL) rice flour

¼ cup (60 mL) corn starch

variety of vegetables and seafood, cut into bite-sized pieces

Heat peanut oil in a pan or deep fryer until temperature is 375° F (190° C). Combine egg, beer and white wine in a small bowl. In another bowl, combine flour, rice flour and cornstarch. Add liquid to dry mixture and very lightly mix together. The batter should look lumpy. Dip vegetables and seafood in tempura batter and fry in small batches until golden and crispy.

Tip
Keys to tasty, crispy tempura are a very light mixing of the batter—lumps are GOOD—and using an ice cold liquid, preferably one that is carbonated. To avoid greasy, soggy tempura, it is important to maintain the proper temperature of the oil, so it's best to have a thermometer on hand.

Tip
For deep-frying, peanut oil should be 2 to 3 inches (5 to 7.5 cm) deep, or use deep fryer according to the manufacturer's directions.

The word tempura comes from the Latin ad tempora cuaresmae, meaning "in the time of Lent." As good Catholics, the Portuguese missionaries substituted fish for meat at this time of the year, and batter-frying was a popular presentation.

Balsamic-glazed Root Vegetables

Serves 4

The term "root vegetable" is used to describe all vegetables grown underground, including potatoes, carrots, onions, rutabagas and beets. Before greenhouses and imported fruits and vegetables, root vegetables were important winter food because they were easy to grow, lasted months in the cellar and were carbohydrate-dense and thus, filling. Today in British Columbia, many of the province's top chefs, who are committed to putting local produce on their tables, are finding new and creative ways to incorporate B.C.'s great winter crop into their menus. This recipe uses the sweetness of reduced balsamic vinegar to enhance the earthy flavours of these winter staples.

Root Vegetables

1 lb (500 g) baby potatoes, a variety if possible, washed and halved or quartered, depending on size

2 medium parsnips, peeled and quartered lengthwise, then halved

1 medium yam, halved then sliced ¼ inch (.5 cm) thick

1 small beet, washed and quartered with skin on

1 large carrot, peeled and quartered lengthwise, then halved

1 bulb garlic, broken into cloves, peeled and left whole

1 small yellow onion, peeled and quartered

Marinade

¼ cup (60 mL) balsamic vinegar

¼ cup (60 mL) extra virgin olive oil or melted butter

2 Tbsp (30 mL) honey

¼ cup (60 mL) fresh parsley, finely chopped

sea salt and freshly ground pepper to taste

2 sprigs fresh thyme

2 sprigs fresh rosemary

Preheat oven to 375° F (190° C). Combine first 4 ingredients of the marinade and set aside.

Place the vegetables into a large mixing bowl. Pour the prepared marinade over top, season with salt and pepper and toss to coat. Place into 13 x 9-inch (33 x 23 cm) pan and assemble the rosemary and thyme sprigs on top. Roast uncovered, turning once or twice, for about 45 minutes or until the edges are golden brown and the vegetables pierce easily with a knife. Toss with fresh parsley and serve as a side dish.

Balsamic vinegar is an aged reduction sauce that originates in the Modena region of Italy. The best balsamic vinegar is aged a long time, comes in very small bottles and is very expensive. Instead, try a cheaper variety, but not the cheapest—it's most likely red vinegar and brown sugar or caramel.

Broccoli and Tempeh Rice Bowl

Serves 4

B.C. is one of the healthiest provinces in Canada, and we have a population that values exercise and healthy eating. This dish combines one of our favourite green vegetables with tempeh, which is similar to tofu and is a staple in many vegetarian diets. Tempeh is made in a similar fashion to tofu using soy beans, but its fermentation process is slightly different, resulting in a stronger flavour, a firmer texture and a higher content of protein, dietary fibre and vitamins. You can find tempeh at many local health food stores or even major grocers such as Whole Foods and Capers. Tempeh's firm texture makes it a good substitute for meat in many recipes.

2 Tbsp (30 mL) soy sauce

1 Tbsp (30 mL) mirin or sweet rice wine

2 Tbsp (30 mL) light miso

1 tsp (5 mL) toasted sesame oil

¼ tsp (1 mL) cornstarch

2 tsp (10 mL) grape seed or canola oil

1 Tbsp (15 mL) ginger, finely chopped

2 tsp (10 mL) lemongrass, tender bottom part only, chopped

2 garlic cloves, minced

1 package Indonesian-style tempeh, cut into ½-inch (1 cm) strips

1 head of broccoli, cut into florets

½ cup (125 mL) each yellow and red pepper, cut into strips

½ cup (125 mL) snow peas

½ cup (125 mL) green onions, cut in ¼-inch (.5 cm) diagonal strips

2 tsp (10 mL) black sesame seeds

½ tsp (2 mL) sea salt

2 cups (500 mL) hot, cooked brown rice

In a small bowl, combine soy sauce, mirin, miso, sesame oil and cornstarch. Stir with a whisk and set aside. Heat oil in a large skillet over medium-high heat and sauté ginger, lemongrass and garlic for 1 minute or just until mixture begins to brown. Add tempeh and sauté for 2 minutes, then add broccoli, peppers, snow peas and sauté for 1 minute. Add reserved mixture to skillet and cook for 1 minute, until sauce has slightly thickened. Remove from heat and stir in green onions, sesame seeds and salt. Serve over rice.

Tip

Soak your broccoli in warm, salted water to get rid of any critters. As with all members of the cabbage family, broccoli is best used within a few days of picking to retain its sweet flavour and mild odour.

Tempeh is a fermented soybean product that has been enjoyed in Southeast Asia for centuries. It is fermented with a Rhizopus mould, which makes the soy protein more easily digestible.

Apple Muffins with Ginger Glaze

Makes 12

These apple muffins pay tribute to the late Father Pandosy, an Oblate missionary who not only planted B.C.'s first vineyard and apple orchard in Kelowna, but who also established the region's first school and Roman Catholic mission in 1860. The Okanagan Valley is still one of Canada's prime apple-growing regions; however, some people are concerned that the success of B.C.'s wine industry could be the demise of this region's famed apples, with many farms replacing orchards with vineyards. Some of the most popular Okanagan apple varieties include Jonagold, Macintosh, Red Delicious and Spartans.

1 Jonagold or Spartan apple

2 cups (500 mL) flour

1 Tbsp (15 mL) baking powder

½ tsp (2 mL) cinnamon

¼ tsp (1 mL) salt

⅓ cup (75 mL) unsalted butter

⅓ cup (75 mL) packed brown sugar

2 large eggs

⅔ cup (150 mL) buttermilk

Glaze

⅓ cup (75 mL) ginger jelly

Preheat oven to 400° F (200° C) and grease a muffin pan. Core and peel apple and cut into ¼-inch (.5 cm) chunks. Into a bowl, sift together flour, baking powder, cinnamon and salt. In a saucepan, melt butter and stir in brown sugar. Remove the pan from the heat and let it cool slightly. Whisk eggs and buttermilk into butter mixture until smooth and add to flour mixture, stirring very lightly until combined. Fold in chunks of apple. Divide batter into the muffin cups and bake for 15 minutes or until golden.

Heat ginger jelly in a small saucepan over low heat until just warm. Brush jam over muffins several times until absorbed for a nice glaze.

Sunflower Granola

The crisp, wholesome nature of granola reflects British Columbia's laid-back, outdoorsy lifestyle. What was once considered the epitome of "hippy food" in the 1960s and a snack food for hikers is now a mainstream breakfast item. A simple mixture of toasted whole grains, nuts and honey, granola can be spruced up with dried B.C. cranberries or blueberries. It is best eaten with yogurt while wearing cosy slippers and poring over the Saturday morning paper. The sunflower seed featured in this granola has been grown commercially in Canada since the early 1940s, but is seen towering over backyards all over the province in summer months.

4 cups (1 L) old-fashioned oats (not quick)

1 cup (250 mL) unsweetened, shredded coconut

1 cup (250 mL) dried fruit of choice: blueberries, cherries, sliced apricots, etc.

1 cup (250 mL) pumpkin seeds

1½ cups (375 mL) sunflower seeds

½ cup (125 mL) sesame seeds

1 cup (250 mL) wheat germ

1 cup (250 mL) chopped almonds

½ cup (125 mL) chopped cashews

⅔ cup (150 mL) maple syrup

1 tsp (5 mL) pure vanilla extract

½ tsp (2 mL) salt

¼ cup (60 mL) sunflower oil

Preheat oven to 325° F (160° C). Place all ingredients in a large bowl and mix well. Spread on a baking sheet and bake for 15 minutes. Stir and bake 10 more minutes. Stir again and bake 5 to 10 minutes more until golden brown. Cool and store in an airtight container for up to a month.

Tip

Sprinkle granola over your favourite cereal or yogurt, or simply enjoy with milk. You can also eat it plain by the handful, or you can freeze it for use at another time.

Sourdough Hotcakes
Makes about 1 dozen

The first leavened breads rose through the action of yeast naturally occurring on the grains and in the air. Before the advent of modern yeast packaging methods, people wanting to bake bread would keep a "starter" containing a proven yeast strain. Prospectors in the San Francisco Gold Rush discovered that their starters were unusually tangy, and the term "sourdough" was born. During a time when food was even more important than money, sourdough was extremely valuable to these prospectors; they used it to feed themselves and their dogs, and the starter was even used to tan hides. It is still popular as a leavening agent today, used by well known bakeries such as La Baguette and Terra Breads at Granville Island.

Quick Sourdough Starter

1 cup (250 mL) water

1 cup (250 mL) unbleached flour

½ tsp (2 mL) active dry yeast

Sourdough Hotcakes

2 cups (500 mL) sourdough starter (see above and opposite)

1½ cups (375 mL) unbleached or wholewheat flour

2 Tbsp (30 mL) sugar, maple syrup or honey

3 Tbsp (45 mL) oil

2 eggs

½ tsp (2 mL) sea salt

1 tsp (5 mL) baking powder

1 tsp (5 mL) baking soda, diluted in 1 Tbsp (15 mL) warm water.

The night before you plan to make hotcakes, mix ingredients well and set out on a countertop in a draft-free area, allowing starter time to develop its characteristic sour taste. Remaining starter can be left on the counter for future use; it is best stored at 65 to 77° F (18 to 25° C). To strengthen and "feed" starter, add ¼ cup (60 mL) water and ½ cup (60 mL) flour every second day.

Sourdough Hotcakes
Preheat griddle or pan to medium-high heat. Mix ingredients, except soda, together. Gently fold in soda and cook cakes right away so as to not lose soda's leavening effect. Serve hot with your favourite condiments.

Old-fashioned Sourdough Starter

Boil unpeeled potatoes until they fall apart. Remove skins. Mash potatoes in a nonmetallic bowl, adding water as needed to make a rich, thick liquid, about 2 cups (500 mL). Add remaining ingredients, beating until smooth, and let stand for 1 week. Feed starter as described opposite for quick starter.

Old-fashioned Sourdough Starter

2 large potatoes

3 Tbsp (45 mL) sugar

1⅔ cups (400 mL) unbleached flour

½ tsp (2 mL) active dry yeast

Cranberry Chutney

Makes 4 cups (1 L)

The word "cranberry" comes from "craneberry"; the flower looks like the head of a crane, and cranes were known to enjoy the berries. Cranberries were a vital food to First Nations people and pioneers because of their naturally occurring benzoic acid, which is a great natural preservative, and their high vitamin C content. Although cranberries are thought of primarily as a Thanksgiving accompaniment, cranberry juice ranks third in sales in North America, after apple and orange. A large percentage of Canada's commercial cranberry crop is grown in southwestern B.C., and it is the province's most economically important berry. Every fall, a cranberry festival is held in Fort Langley.

1 Tbsp (15 mL) unsalted butter

8 oz (250 g) pearl onions or cipollini (small, flattened Italian variety), peeled and left whole

2 Tbsp (30 mL) grated ginger

1 serrano chili, minced

2 kaffir lime leaves or 1 Tbsp (15 mL) lime zest

2¼ cups (560 mL) apple cider vinegar

1 cup (250 mL) light brown sugar

1 cup (250 mL) muscovado sugar

2 lbs (1 kg) fresh cranberries

¾ cup (175 mL) dried fruit such as currants, cranberries, blueberries or sour cherries

sea salt and freshly ground pepper

In a medium-sized pot, melt butter and sauté onions over medium heat for 5 minutes. Add next 6 ingredients and bring to a boil. Add cranberries and dried fruit, turn heat to medium-low and simmer for about 15 minutes or until chutney is thick and has reduced.

Season with salt and pepper, and refrigerate until well chilled.

Tip
Instead of cranberries in this recipe, you could use mango, rhubarb, apple, pear or peach—or experiment using a variety of fruits.

Nanaimo Bars

Makes 12 squares

Nanaimo is a picturesque community on central Vancouver Island. The Nanaimo District Museum receives so many inquiries into the origins of the Nanaimo bar that it is considering developing an exhibit in honour of this sinful treat. There are at least three similar bar recipes from the early 1950s. One, called "chocolate slice," appeared in *The Women's Auxiliary to the Nanaimo Hospital Cook Book* (1952); a second, published in the *Vancouver Sun*, was called "Nanaimo Bars"; a third version, "Mrs. Gayton's Bars," was printed in a 1955 cookbook from St. Aidan's United Church in Victoria. There is even a place in Nanaimo that has taken decadence to a whole new level with its "Deep Fried Nanaimo Bar".

Layer 1

½ cup (125 mL) butter

¼ cup (60 mL) sugar

2 Tbsp (30 mL) cocoa

1 egg

2 cups (500 g) graham cracker crumbs

1 cup (250 mL) shredded coconut

½ cup (125 mL) toasted, chopped nuts of your choice

1 tsp (5 mL) pure vanilla extract

Layer 2

¼ cup (60 mL) half and half cream (10–18%)

2 Tbsp (30 mL) custard powder

3 Tbsp (45 mL) butter

1 tsp (5 mL) pure vanilla extract

2 cups (500 mL) sifted icing sugar

Layer 3

5 oz (140 g) semi-sweet chocolate

2 Tbsp (30 mL) butter

Layer 1

Soften butter in a double boiler, add sugar, cocoa and egg and then heat until slightly thickened. Stir in rest of ingredients, and press mixture into a 9-inch (23 cm) square pan. Chill 15 minutes.

Layer 2

Mix ingredients together and spread evenly over first layer. Chill 15 minutes.

Layer 3

Melt chocolate and butter together until smooth and spread over second layer. Chill 15 minutes. Score top with a sharp knife to make 12 squares, then cut and serve or store in an airtight container for up to 1 week.

Espresso Nanimo Bars

Add 2 tsp (10 mL) instant espresso powder and 2 Tbsp (30 mL) heavy cream (32%) to second layer. Once third layer has been spread, stud centre of each square with a chocolate-covered coffee bean. Chill, cut and serve.

Pistachio Ginger Nanaimo Bars

(featured in photo) Use ½ cup (125 mL) chopped, unsalted pistachios as nuts in first layer. When second layer is cool, spread 1 cup (250 mL) of finely diced candied ginger over it, then pour third layer overtop. Chill, cut and serve.

Hazelnut Torte with Okanagan Sour Cherry Preserve

Serves 10 to 12

Hazelnuts are the only nut crop commercially produced in B.C., with more than 660,000 pounds (300,000 kilograms) produced annually. The majority of the hazelnut farms are located in the Fraser Valley, where producers press the nuts for their oil or grind them into flour as well as sell them whole. Joy Road Organics has created an Okanagan Sour Cherry Preserve that is one of the best in the province, using organically grown cherries from the Naramata Bench region. With its pure, syrupy flavour, this preserve is a fantastic contrast to the hazelnut torte. By combining these two unique ingredients, you have a truly B.C. dessert!

2 cups (500 mL) cake flour

2 tsp (10 mL) baking powder

1/2 tsp (2 mL) salt

6 egg yolks

1/2 cup (125 mL) canola oil

1/2 cup (125 mL) water

1 cup (250 mL) sugar

6 egg whites

1 cup (250 mL) hazelnuts, chopped and toasted

1/4 cup (60 mL) strong brewed coffee, cooled

1 cup (250 mL) heavy cream (32%)

6 oz (170 g) bittersweet chocolate, chopped

1 x 14 oz (400 g) jar of Nutella chocolate hazelnut spread

toasted hazelnuts for garnish

1 x 8 oz (250 mL) jar of sour cherry preserve

Preheat oven to 350° F (175° C). Grease and lightly flour two 9-inch (23 cm) springform pans. Combine flour, baking powder and salt in a bowl and set aside. In a large mixing bowl, beat egg yolks, oil, water and sugar with an electric mixer on medium speed for 5 minutes, scraping bowl occasionally. Fold in flour mixture.

In another large mixing bowl, beat egg whites with an electric mixer on medium to high speed until soft peaks form. Gently fold about 1 cup (250 mL) of egg white mixture into egg yolk mixture. Fold the rest of the egg yolk mixture into remaining egg white mixture. Then fold in the chopped hazelnuts. Spoon the batter evenly into prepared pans. Bake in oven for 20 minutes or until a toothpick inserted in the centre comes out clean. Immediately poke holes all over the cakes with a toothpick and drizzle coffee evenly over. Let the cakes cool on wire racks for 10 minutes before removing from pans. When they have cooled completely, slice in half horizontally.

In a medium saucepan, heat whipping cream to simmer. Remove from heat and add bittersweet chocolate, stirring until melted. Reserve 1/4 cup (60 mL) of chocolate mixture for drizzling; cover and set aside. Cool remaining chocolate mixture to room temperature, for about an hour. Transfer mixture to medium bowl and beat with an electric mixer on medium speed for 3 minutes or until it is thickened. Spread chocolate filling evenly on 3 cake layers, and frost the top and sides with chocolate hazelnut spread. Drizzle the reserved chocolate on top and garnish with toasted hazelnuts. Serve with sour cherry preserve on the side.

For all types of nuts, a 3.5 oz. (100 g) serving has 550 to 700 calories and contains protein, phosphorus and potassium.

INDEX